Everyday FOLK ART

Hooked Rugs and Quilts to Make

POLLY MINICK and
LAURIE SIMPSON

Martingale®
& COMPANY

Everyday Folk Art:
Hooked Rugs and Quilts to Make
© 2005 by Polly Minick and Laurie Simpson

That Patchwork Place® is an imprint
of Martingale & Company®.

Martingale & Company
20205 144th Avenue NE
Woodinville, WA 98072-8478 USA
www.martingale-pub.com

Credits

President: Nancy J. Martin
CEO: Daniel J. Martin
VP and General Manager: Tom Wierzbicki
Publisher: Jane Hamada
Editorial Director: Mary V. Green
Managing Editor: Tina Cook
Technical Editor: Karen Costello Soltys
Copy Editor: Melissa Bryan
Design Director: Stan Green
Illustrator: Robin Strobel
Cover and Text Designer: Stan Green
Photographer: Brent Kane

Mission Statement
Dedicated to providing quality products
and service to inspire creativity.

Printed in China
10 09 08 07 06 05   8 7 6 5 4 3 2 1

Library of Congress Cataloging-in-Publication Data

Minick, Polly.
    Everyday folk art : hooked rugs and quilts to
make / Polly Minick and Laurie Simpson.
        p. cm.
    Includes bibliographical references.
    ISBN 1-56477-558-5 (alk. paper)
    1. Rugs, Hooked—Patterns. 2. Hooking.
3. Patchwork—Patterns. 4. Quilting. 5. Quilts.
I. Simpson, Laurie. II. Title.
    TT850.M53 2005
    746.7′4—dc22

                                            2004023947

Contents

Introduction ~ 5

STARS GALORE ~ 8
LeMoyne Star String Quilt ~ 11
White Stars Rug ~ 17

GAME BOARD ~ 20
Game Board Quilt ~ 23
Game Board Rug ~ 29

FOLKY ANIMALS ~ 32
Folky Animals Quilt ~ 35
Folky Cats Rug ~ 41

RUSTIC CABINS ~ 44
Log Cabin Quilt ~ 47
Log Cabin Rug with Quilt-Block Border ~ 55

ANCHORS AWEIGH ~ 59
Sailor Penny Rug ~ 61
Patriotic Shield Rug ~ 69

IRISH CHAIN ~ 72
Snow Day Quilt ~ 75
Irish Chain Rug ~ 85

MARINER'S COMPASS ~ 88
Nautical Wool Quilt ~ 91
Mariner's Compass Rug ~ 97

AMERICA'S PASTIME ~ 100
Baseball Quilt ~ 103
Baseball Rug ~ 113

Quiltmaking Basics ~ 116
Rug-Hooking Basics ~ 126
Resources ~ 142
Acknowledgments ~ 143
About the Authors ~ 144

FRANK J. MIELE
CONTEMPORARY AMERICAN FOLK ART
gallery
at
★ C★UNTRY C★RNER ★

**TAKE ME OUT TO
THE BALLGAME**

America's pastime is celebrated
in an exhibition of
Hooked rugs by Polly Minick
and
Quilts by Laurie Simpson

March 30 through April 25
ARTISTS' RECEPTION: THURSDAY, APRIL 1, 6 TO 9PM

1086 Madison Avenue (at 82nd Street) New York 212.249.7250
www.americanFOLKart.com

Introduction

Creating our own quilts and hand-hooked rugs is our passion. In this, our second collection of folk-art projects, we hope to inspire you to fulfill your own passion. We have been collectors and makers of folk art for most of our lives. While one of us still doesn't sew a stitch, and the other hasn't learned to hook, we find our art forms have a similar graphic and tactile appeal—and they complement one another perfectly in our homes. We've been sharing our ideas and projects with each other for years, even though we live over 1,000 miles apart. For a while now we have known how well rugs and quilts work together, and since the publication of our first book, *Folk Art Friends*, we have heard how much you agree.

In earlier years, quilting and rug hooking were essential for addressing the needs and comforts of Americans and others around the world. Today we are helping transform activities that were once basic and fundamentally vital for existence into art forms that are functional and also loved for their aesthetic qualities. We feel that rug hooking and quilting represent the epitome of fiber art. In this book we will share our personal style and how-to techniques for 16 projects. The lovely photographs of the projects plus ones of additional quilts and rugs we've made will inspire you to give your quilts and rugs a prominent place in your home. We hope you find *Everyday Folk Art* to be both instructional and inspirational—whether you are a novice or an experienced fiber artist.

Everyday household objects created by self-taught artists—that is what folk art means to us, whether the objects are carved weathervanes, painted tin boxes, or hand-crafted quilts and rugs. The projects in this book convey our personal interpretation of folk art. You'll find that the items in our pairs of projects complement each other yet have their own unique qualities. The inspiration can come from many sources. A conversation about the many baseball players and fans in our family was the source of inspiration for our baseball-themed quilts and rug (shown opposite and on pages 102 and 112). A stunning antique game board collection served as another muse. One of us would start with a sketch or a collection of wool or cotton fabrics, and the other would follow. Inspiration can come from anywhere, and soon you will notice it all around you.

Our hope is that you will come away with many rewards: the knowledge and confidence to make your own projects shine; creative ideas for decorating with rugs and quilts; and a newfound appreciation for both of these age-old crafts as important art forms for today.

Polly McKillen Minick

Laurie McKillen Simpson

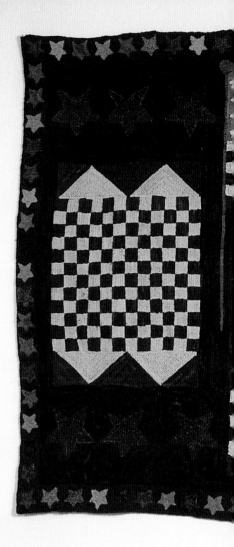

A collection of antique painted wooden game boards was the inspiration for Polly's large game board rug.

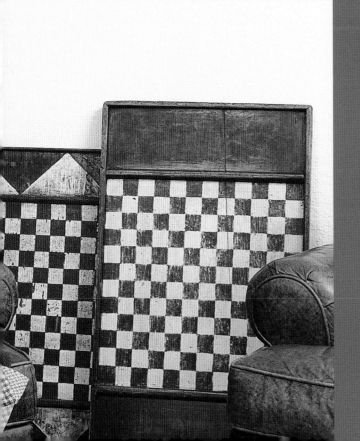

Stars Galore

I have collected reproduction fabrics since I started quilting. This indigo-and-shirting quilt helped put a dent in my stash. A timeless pattern and lots of scraps make a "can't-miss" combo.

Laurie Simpson

Star rugs have always been among my favorites, ever since I began designing them in the late 1970s. I have made this style of rug in a few variations and sizes, but the stars were always black. Now, after moving south and making major color changes in my decorating scheme, I instantly got inspired to do my favorite star pattern in off-whites and many shades of blue.

Polly Minick

8

Finished Quilt Size: 67" x 87" • Finished Block Size: 18"

LeMoyne Star String Quilt

Materials

Yardages are based on 42"-wide fabric.

• 8 yards total of assorted white and beige fabrics for star blocks and border

• 12 fat quarters of assorted indigo prints for block backgrounds

• 2½ yards of indigo fabric for borders and binding

• 5½ yards of backing fabric

• 68" x 88" piece of batting

• Paper for foundation piecing (100-sheet package)

Cutting

All measurements include ¼"-wide seam allowances.

This string-pieced quilt will use up all of your white and beige scraps—and then some!

From the white and beige fabrics, cut:
    • Strips in assorted widths of 1" to 4"; strips can be of any length
    • 2"-wide strips for border; strips can be of random length

From *each* of the indigo fat quarters, cut:
- 4 squares, 5¾" x 5¾" (12 matching sets of 4 each)
- 1 square, 8¾" x 8¾"; cut squares in half twice diagonally to yield 48 triangles

From the indigo fabric, cut:
- 2 border strips, 3½" x 72½"
- 2 border strips, 4½" x 60½"
- 2 border strips, 2½" x 83½"
- 2 border strips, 2½" x 67½"
- 8 binding strips, 2¼" x 42"
- Approximately 20 assorted 2" x 2" squares or 1½" x 2" pieces for border

Making the LeMoyne Star Blocks

You will need 12 LeMoyne Star blocks.

1. Photocopy the star-point foundation pattern from page 15 onto the sheets of foundation paper. Repeat to make 96 copies. Make sure the reproductions are dark enough so that the diamond outlines show through to the wrong side of the paper. You can trace this outline with a pencil onto the other side if this is helpful. The tracing doesn't have to be perfect—you just want to know roughly where the diamond shape is.

2. On the sewing machine, foundation piece the white and beige assorted-width strips to the wrong side of the paper. (The original diamond shape you made on the copy machine is now on the underneath side of the paper.) Begin by laying the first strip of fabric right side up (wrong side against the paper) and then laying the next strip on top of the first strip, right sides together and

with one long edge aligned with a long edge of the first strip. Stitch approximately ¼" from the raw edges of the strips.

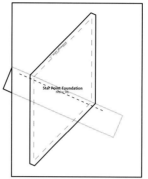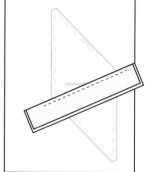

Position fabric beneath printed paper.

Stitch from this side.

3. Flip the top strip open so that both strips are right side up. Press. Continue adding strips of random widths, aligning the edge of each new strip with the last strip added, until the entire diamond shape is covered. Press after the addition of each strip. Make a total of 96 foundation-pieced diamonds.

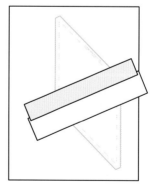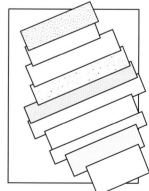

4. Turn each stitched diamond so that the fabric side is down on your cutting mat. Use a ruler and rotary cutter to trim away the excess paper, making sure to leave a ¼" seam allowance.

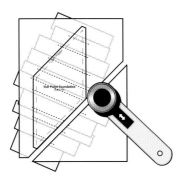

5. If you plan to piece the diamonds together by hand, gently tear the paper off the back of each diamond, taking care not to distort the shape. The paper will tear more easily if you crease it first along the seam line. If you plan to assemble the blocks by machine, you can leave the paper patterns on the diamonds for now and remove them after all the block pieces have been stitched together.

6. Either by hand or by machine, piece together the LeMoyne Star block. First sew diamonds together in pairs, ending the seam ¼" from the outer end of the diamonds. Sew the pairs together to make half stars, and then sew the halves

together, again leaving the last ¼" of each seam open.

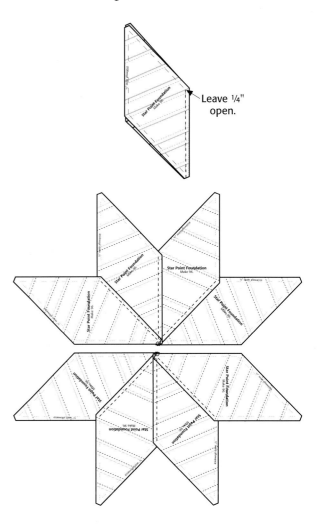

Leave ¼" open.

7. Select four matching indigo squares and triangles. Sew the corner squares and side triangles in place, leaving the seam allowances free in the corners where the squares and triangles adjoin with two diamonds.

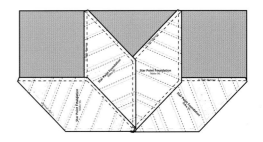

8. Sew the two halves of the star block together, again leaving the seam allowances free in the corners where the triangles will be added. Sew the two remaining indigo triangles in place and then press the block.

9. Repeat steps 6 and 7 to make a total of 12 LeMoyne Star blocks.

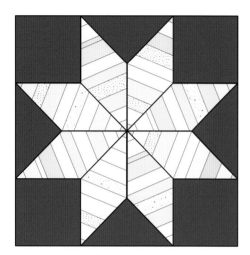

LeMoyne Star Block
Make 12.

10. Arrange the blocks in four rows of three blocks each. When you are pleased with the arrangement, sew the blocks together into rows, and then sew the rows together. Press.

Adding the Borders

1. Sew a 3½" x 72½" indigo strip to each side of the quilt. Press the seam allowances toward the border strips. Sew the 4½" x 60½" indigo strips to the top and bottom of the quilt. Press the seam allowances toward the outside edge.

2. To make the middle borders, sew the 2"-wide strips of white or beige and the assorted indigo scraps together in a random manner to make four border strips. Make two strips at least 85" long and two at least 62" long.

3. Attach the two longest strips to the sides of the quilt top. Trim the strips even with the finished edges of the top. Press the seam allowances toward the indigo border strips. Attach the other two strips to the top and bottom of the quilt top, and trim and press in the same manner.

4. Sew the 2½" x 83½" indigo strips to the sides of the quilt top. Press the seam allowances toward the outer indigo strips. Sew the 2½" x 67½" strips to the top and bottom of the quilt top. Press in the same manner.

Finishing the Quilt

1. Choose a quilting design and then follow the directions for marking the quilt top as described in "Quiltmaking Basics" on page 123.

2. From the backing fabric, cut two pieces, 95" long. Remove the selvages and join the pieces to make a 75" x 95" backing piece. Press the seam allowances open.

3. Center and layer the quilt top and batting over the backing; baste the layers together and then quilt as desired. The quilt shown was hand quilted with a series of concentric stars within each of the large string stars and feathered wreaths within the large blue spaces where four block corners meet.

4. Trim the batting and backing even with the quilt top. Use the 2¼" x 42" indigo strips to bind the quilt, referring to page 124 as needed.

5. Make a label and attach it to the back of your quilt.

¼" seam allowance

Star-Point Foundation
Make 96.

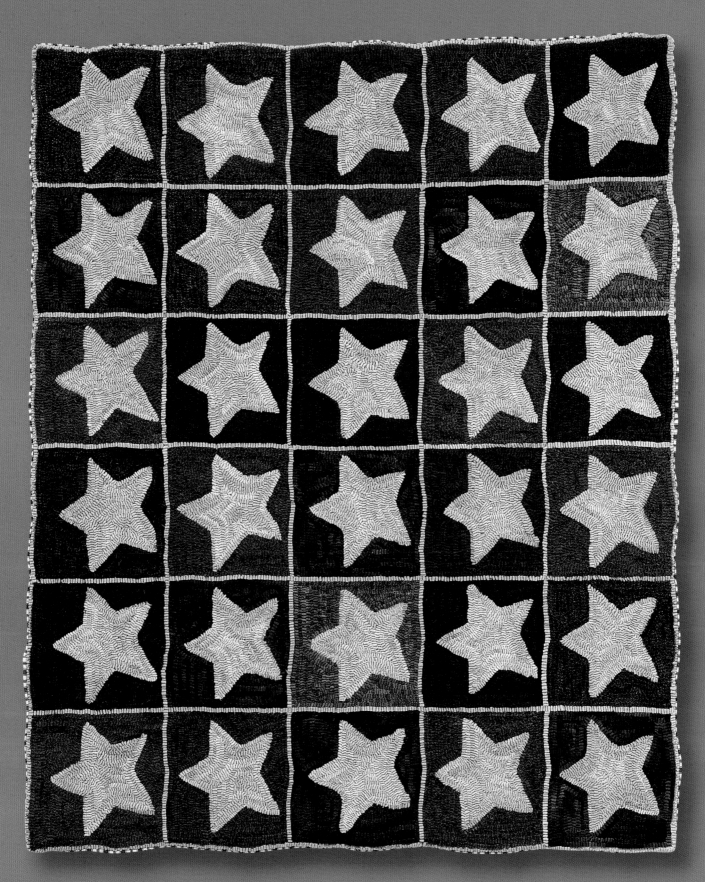

Finished Rug Size: 37³/₄" x 45¹/₄"

White Stars Rug

Materials

Wool yardages are estimated based on 60"-wide fabric. (See "How Much Wool Do You Need?" on page 133 for more information on estimating yardage before beginning any project.)

• 1½ to 2 yards total of various off-white wools for stars

• ¼ yard each of 20 different blue wools for background (or whatever color you chose for your rug)

• 43" x 52" piece of backing fabric*

• 185" of binding tape *or* ⅓ yard of vintage ticking fabric as used on this rug

*If you use a hoop, add 8" to the backing measurements. See "Rug Backing" on page 132 for more information on fabric-measuring techniques and backing options.

Cutting

Cut your wool into size #8 or #9 strips, referring to "Cutting the Strips" on page 133. I recommend not cutting all the wool at once; it is prone to tangle into worms. However, be sure to cut some strips from each of the various off-whites so that you can mix them up for better texture as you hook each star.

Making the Rug

1. Transfer the design onto your backing fabric, using the pattern (which needs to be enlarged 600%) on page 19. For details on transferring patterns, see page 132 in "Rug-Hooking Basics." Then either serge or zigzag around the edges by machine or encase the edges in masking tape to prevent raveling as you hook the rug.

2. Outline and fill each star using a mixture of all the off-white wools that you have cut into strips. Choose them randomly for a nice effect.

3. Hook single rows of loops to create the white outlines that separate the blue squares.

4. Fill the background areas around each star using the various shades of blue (or whatever color you chose for your rug).

Color Planning Your Rug

The project directions call for 20 different pieces of blue wool to achieve the look of the rug shown. If you don't have that many different shades, don't worry. You can repeat a few of the blues, but plan to have some variety because it's the multiple shades of blue that give this rug its extra visual interest. Of course, you may choose a different color for your background, but try to follow the rule of ¼ yard of background color for each block, and for a pleasant look, use as many shades of the same color (that do not fight with each other) as possible.

Finishing the Rug

1. Finish your rug using binding tape or vintage ticking fabric as shown here. (For tips on tape application and other finishing options, see "Finishing Your Rug" on page 138.)

2. Steam and block the rug, referring to "Blocking" on page 139.

3. Sew on an identification tag, referring to "Signing Your Rug" on page 140 for various options.

White Stars Rug
37¾" x 45¼"
1 square = ½"
Enlarge pattern 600%.

Game Board

When I hooked the large game board rug on page 6, Laurie was intrigued. She has always been taken with a Parcheesi board that hangs on the wall in our home. Armed with just a photograph, she designed and made her Game Board quilt. I was so impressed with it that I decided I had to hook one more game board to accompany Laurie's beautiful quilt.

❧ Polly Minick ❧

Polly's game board collection was the inspiration for these projects. Quilt designs are everywhere!

❧ Laurie Simpson ❧

20

Finished Quilt Size: 46" x 46" • Finished Block Size: 12"

Game Board Quilt

Materials

Yardages are based on 42"-wide fabric.

• 1½ yards total of assorted light khaki fabrics for blocks and inner border

• 1⅛ yards total of assorted purple fabrics for blocks, outer border, and binding

• ½ yard total of assorted red fabrics for blocks

• ¼ yard total of assorted terra cotta fabrics for blocks

• ¼ yard total of assorted blue fabrics for blocks

• ¼ yard or scraps of dark khaki fabric for blocks

• 3 yards of backing fabric

• 50" x 50" piece of batting

Cutting

All measurements include ¼"-wide seam allowances. The patterns for the star pieces are on page 27.

From the light khaki fabrics, cut:
- • 2 border strips, 1" x 36½"
- • 2 border strips, 1" x 37½"
- • 16 pieces, 4½" x 5"
- • 16 pieces, 2" x 2"
- • 5 of star point A
- • 4 of star border C
- • 25 of star background B

From the red fabrics, cut:
- • 32 rectangles, 2" x 4½"
- • 8 pieces, 1½" x 2"
- • 5 of star point A
- • 4 of star border C

From the terra cotta fabrics, cut:
- 5 of star point A
- 4 of star border C

From the blue fabrics, cut:
- 5 of star point A
- 4 of star border C

From the purple fabrics, cut:
- 2 border strips, 5" x 36½"
- 2 border strips, 5" x 37½"
- 4 pieces, 5" x 5½"
- 5 binding strips, 2¼" x 42"
- 5 of star point A
- 4 of star border C

From the dark khaki fabric, cut:
- 8 rectangles, 2" x 4½"

Making the Star Blocks

You will need five blocks in the following color combinations: red star with terra cotta border, terra cotta star with red border, blue star with purple border, purple star with blue border, and light khaki star with light khaki border.

1. Sew a khaki B piece to the right side of a star point. Begin stitching ¼" from the wide-angle corner of the star. Backstitch and sew all the way to the end of the seam. Repeat four more times using the same color of star points. Press the seam allowances in one direction.

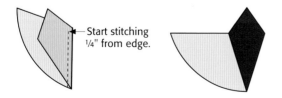

Start stitching ¼" from edge.

2. Sew all five sections together. Note that you will need to set in the seams where two star points and one background piece come together. To do so, start and stop sewing ¼" from the edge of the pieces, allowing the seam allowance to remain free of stitching. You may find it easiest to do this if you sew from the inner point of the star toward the outer edge. Press all of the seam allowances in one direction.

3. Piece together the four same-colored star border pieces, taking care not to stretch the pieces. (The entire concave curve is cut on the bias, so it stretches easily if you're not careful.)

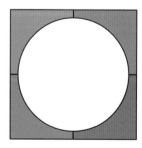

4. On the wrong side of the center star unit, mark four dots on the seam allowances at north, south, east, and west. To accurately mark these four points, choose one star point to be north, and then fold the circle in half horizontally so that the north point is midway

between the two bottom star points. Mark south directly below north and then mark east and west at the fold line.

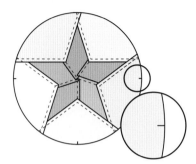

5. Matching the seams of the star border to these marked dots, stitch the star to the border. If piecing by machine, stitch slowly, gently easing the fabric as necessary as you round the curve, and taking care not to stretch the fabric or stitch pleats into the border fabric.

Easy Does It

Piecing this star into its border is just like piecing a Drunkard's Path block—only times four. Match the dots to the seams in the border and then ease in the star all around. Pin at the halfway point between the dots and then again halfway between the pins.

6. Repeat steps 1–5 to make each of the star blocks. Carefully press the seams toward the outside, taking care not to stretch the bias seams.

Making the Red and Khaki Blocks

1. Sew a 2" x 2" light khaki piece to each end of a 1½" x 2" red piece. Repeat to make a total of eight units. Press the seams in one direction.

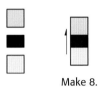

Make 8.

2. Sew a 4½" x 5" light khaki piece to each side of the units made in step 1 along the 4½" edge. Sew a 2" x 4½" dark khaki rectangle to one end of each unit as shown. Press the seam allowances in one direction.

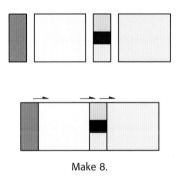

Make 8.

3. Sew together eight of the 2" x 4½" red rectangles along the long edges as shown. Repeat to make a total of four red strips. Press the seam allowances in one direction.

Make 4.

4. Sew a khaki unit to each side of the red units, making sure that both dark khaki rectangles are at the same end of the block. Press the seam allowances in one direction.

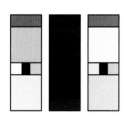 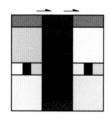

Make 4.

Assembling the Quilt Top

1. Lay out the nine blocks as shown in the quilt photograph on page 22. Sew the blocks together into rows, and then sew the rows together. Press.

2. Sew a 1" x 36½" light khaki strip to a 5" x 36½" purple strip. Repeat. Press the seam allowances toward the purple strips. Sew these to the right and left sides of the quilt top. Press the seam allowances toward the outside edges.

3. Sew a 1" x 37½" light khaki strip to a 5" x 37½" purple strip. Repeat. Press the seam allowances toward the purple strips. Sew a 5" x 5½" purple piece to each end of these strips. Press the seam allowances toward the outside. Attach these top and bottom borders to the

quilt top. Press the seam allowances toward the borders.

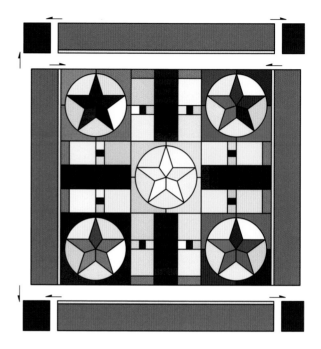

Finishing the Quilt

1. Choose a quilting design and then follow the directions for marking the quilt top as described in "Quiltmaking Basics" on page 123.

2. From the backing fabric, cut two pieces, 26" x 51". Remove the selvages and join the pieces to make a 51" x 51" backing piece. Press the seam allowances open.

3. Center and layer the quilt top and batting over the backing; baste the layers together and then quilt as desired. The quilt shown was hand quilted in a pattern of overlapping concentric circles.

4. Trim the batting and backing even with the edges of the quilt top. Use the 2¼" x 42" purple strips to bind the quilt, referring to page 124 as needed.

5. Make a label and attach it to the back of your quilt.

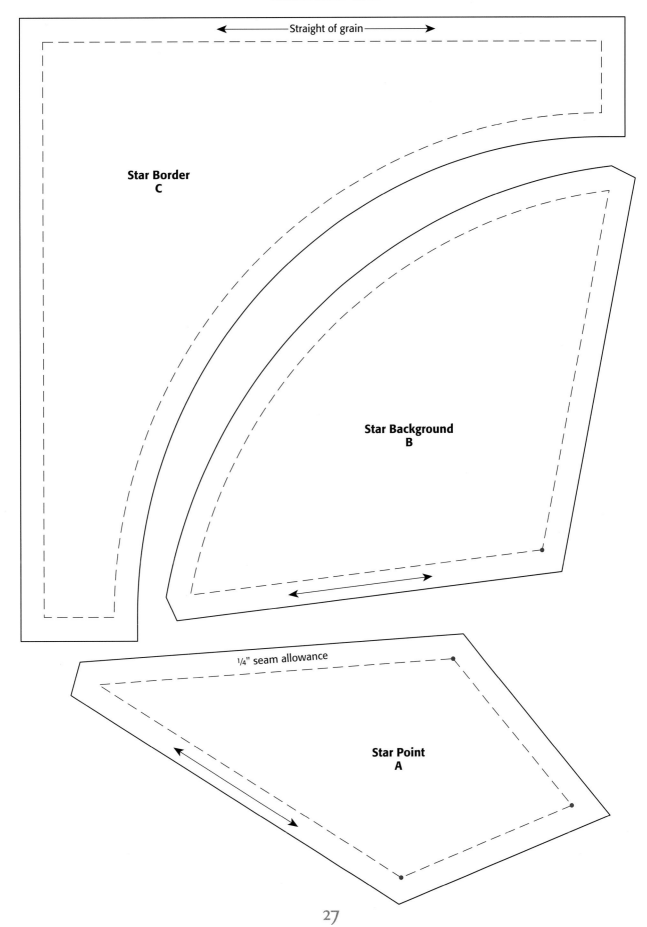

Straight of grain

Star Border
C

Star Background
B

¼" seam allowance

Star Point
A

Finished Rug Size: 37" x 37"

Game Board Rug

Materials

Wool yardages are estimated based on 60"-wide fabric. (See "How Much Wool Do You Need?" on page 133 for more information on estimating yardage before beginning any project.)

• 1½ yards total of cream, off-white, and beige wools for star, star background, and bars

• 1 yard total of assorted old-red wools for bars and star background (See dye formula for Polly's Favorite Red on page 131.)

• ¾ yard total of assorted purple wools for star, star border, and rug border

• ½ yard total of assorted bright blue wools for star and star border

• ½ yard total of assorted brighter red wools for star and star border

• ½ yard total of assorted darker red wools for star and star border

• ½ yard total of assorted terra cotta wools for star and star border

• ½ yard total of assorted mustard wools for block outlines and small rectangles

• 43" x 43" piece of backing fabric*

• 180" of binding tape *or* ¼ yard of striped fabric as used in this rug

*If you use a hoop, add 8" to the backing measurements. See "Rug Backing" on page 132 for more information on fabric-measuring techniques and backing options.

Cutting

Cut your wool into size #8 or #9 strips, referring to "Cutting the Strips" on page 133. I recommend not cutting all the wool at once; it is prone to tangle into worms. However, if you are using a variety of creamy off-whites as I did, make sure you cut some of each shade and randomly use a mix of the pieces as you hook.

Making the Rug

1. Transfer the design onto your backing fabric, using the pattern (which needs to be enlarged 500%) on page 31. For details on transferring patterns, see page 132 in "Rug-Hooking Basics." Then either serge or zigzag around the edges by machine or encase the edges in masking tape to prevent raveling as you hook the rug.

2. Begin hooking in the center of the rug, hooking the light star first. The center star has very low contrast, but the direction of the hooking as well as slight differences in the light wool colors will make the star visible. For each star point, hook just inside the outline first, and then fill in. Next, create the circle that surrounds the star by hooking one wedge shape at a time. Hook the arc of the wedge first, and then fill in. Finally, hook the border area of the block with the darkest of your light wools. The tone-on-tone look is subtle, but I like the way it turns out.

3. After the center block is hooked, do the mustard outlines of the off-white rectangular areas and the small mustard rectangles in the center of each large rectangle. Then fill in the red strips and off-white strips in the four blocks that do not have stars. The red border is a mixture of as many reds as I could find in that color range, giving added interest to the rug. Notice how the reds are hooked in from side to side within the column, while the off-white rectangles are hooked from end to end. This difference in hooking direction adds to the overall texture of the completed rug.

4. I hooked the corner blocks last because I knew their greater variety of colors would be fun to work with. Like the accompanying quilt on page 23, this project uses different shades of blues, purples, terra cottas, and reds for the stars and the star borders. The wedges that make up the circles are also varied slightly to resemble the quilt and give the rug a nice look.

5. Finally, hook the outside border. I used purples left over from one of the stars to hook a two-row border.

Finishing the Rug

1. Finish your rug using binding tape or fabric such as the purple stripe shown here. (For tips on tape application and other finishing options, see "Finishing Your Rug" on page 138.)

2. Steam and block your rug, referring to "Blocking" on page 139.

3. Sew on an identification tag, referring to "Signing Your Rug" on page 140 for various options.

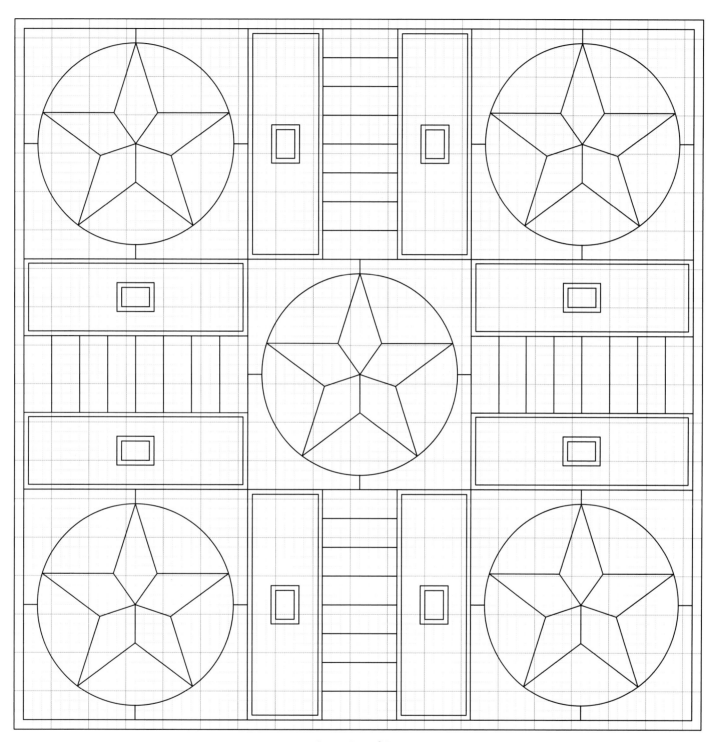

Game Board Rug
37" x 37"
1 square = ½"
Enlarge pattern 500%.

Folky Animals

Laurie and I were inspired by an antique textile owned by our cousin, Patty Tracey. We kept looking it over, because it is a most unusual early piece depicting many folk-style animals. Laurie and I were moved by the work and we each decided to interpret it in our own way. Laurie was drawn to do more than one animal, and I could not get past the idea of the folk-art cat. This is my adaptation of the early piece.

❧ Polly Minick ❧

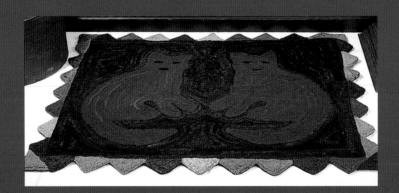

Patty's folk-art piece is one of my favorite things in my cousin's exquisite home. Graciously, she let Polly and me improvise from it. Thanks, Patty!

❧ Laurie Simpson ❧

Finished Quilt Size: 50" x 31"
(including prairie points)

Folky Animals Quilt

Materials

Yardages are based on 42"-wide fabric.

- 29½" x 48½" piece of brown wool for background

- 16" x 23" piece of blue wool for large cat

- 15" x 19" piece of gold wool for dog

- 10" x 15" piece of black wool for small and medium cats

- 7" x 10" piece of red wool for small cat

- 90 squares, 3" x 3", of assorted cotton prints for prairie points

- Spool of linen thread

- 4 skeins of needlepoint wool or embroidery floss in blacks and grays

- 35" x 54" piece of backing fabric

- 33" x 52" piece of batting

Cutting

Enlarge the patterns 250% on pages 37–39, and then cut the animals out of the wool. A good way to mark on wool is with a Sharpie permanent marker. Cut inside the marked line so that no ink remains on the finished piece. A Sharpie with metallic silver ink works well on dark wool, and a black permanent marker works adequately on the rest.

Assembling the Quilt Top

1. Lay out the animals on the brown wool quilt top in a pleasing manner and appliqué them in place using the blanket stitch. (See "Embroidery Details" on page 123 for blanket-stitch how-to.) After each application, steam press the top to help the appliquéd pieces lie flat.

2. Using the linen thread and a running stitch, stitch the cats' eyes, noses, and one mouth.

3. Press each 3" cotton square in half twice diagonally to make the prairie points.

Prairie Point
Make 90.

4. Lay the prairie points along the edges of the quilt so that the raw edges of the prairie points are even with the raw edge of the quilt. Insert the folded point of one triangle into the open point of the one adjacent to it. Continue positioning them all the way around the quilt, adjusting them by eye until you are pleased with the spacing. Pin them in place.

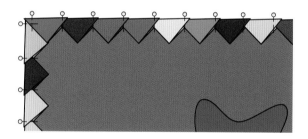

5. Set your sewing machine to a long stitch length and sew the prairie points into place along the raw edge. The points should remain unattached on the folded edge.

Finishing the Quilt

1. Center and layer the quilt top and batting over the backing; baste the layers together.

2. Quilt as desired using the linen thread and a large embroidery or chenille needle. The quilting motion is exactly as if using a smaller quilting needle; your stitches will simply be larger, allowing them to show on the higher-loft wool fabric. Move the prairie points out of the way as you quilt near them. Leave a ½" margin unquilted all the way around the perimeter of the quilt.

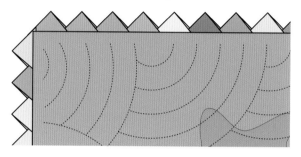

3. Trim the quilt batting exactly to the edge of the quilt top. Trim the backing so that it is ½" larger all around than the quilt top.

4. Fold the prairie points up and tuck their raw edges over the edge of the batting. Then turn under the raw edges of the quilt backing ½" toward the inside of the quilt to encase the prairie point edges and batting. Whipstitch the backing in place.

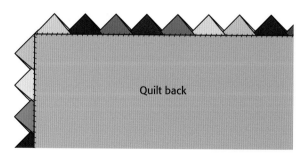

Quilt back

5. Make a label and attach it to the back of your quilt.

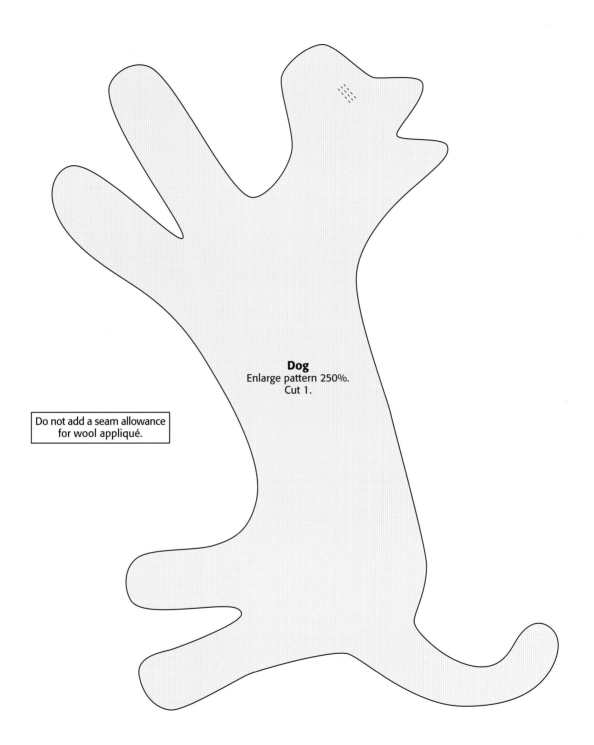

Dog
Enlarge pattern 250%.
Cut 1.

Do not add a seam allowance
for wool appliqué.

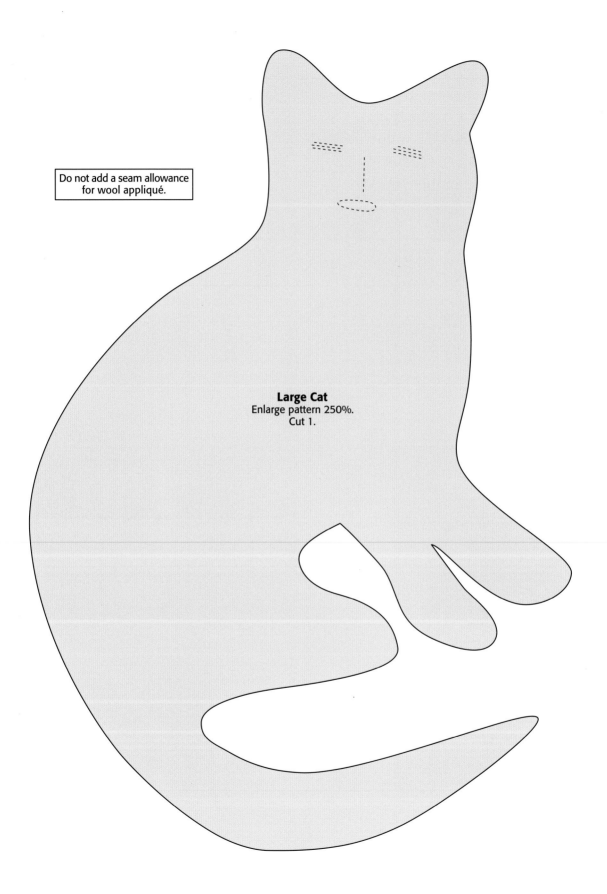

Do not add a seam allowance
for wool appliqué.

Large Cat
Enlarge pattern 250%.
Cut 1.

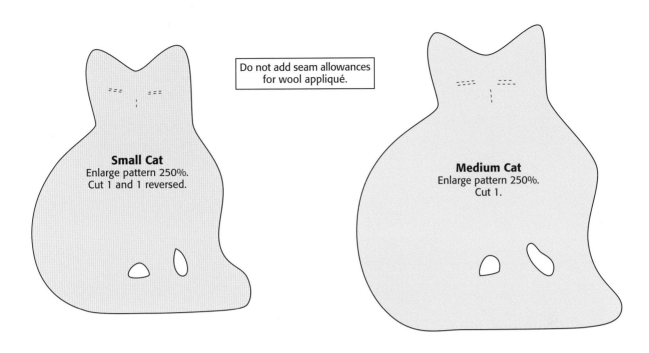

Do not add seam allowances
for wool appliqué.

Small Cat
Enlarge pattern 250%.
Cut 1 and 1 reversed.

Medium Cat
Enlarge pattern 250%.
Cut 1.

Finished Rug Size: 38" x 30"

Folky Cats Rug

Materials

Wool yardages are estimated based on 60"-wide fabric. (See "How Much Wool Do You Need?" on page 133 for more information on estimating yardage before beginning any project.)

• 1½ yards total of royal blue wools for cats

• 1½ yards total of antique brown-black wools for background and cats' eyes and mouths

• 36 strips, 4" x 16", in assorted colors of wool for points

• 46" x 38" piece of backing fabric*

• 220" of binding tape *or* fabric as on this rug

*If you use a hoop, add 8" to the backing measurements. See "Rug Backing" on page 132 for more information on fabric-measuring techniques and backing options.

Cutting

Cut your wool into size #8 or #9 strips, referring to "Cutting Your Strips" on page 133. I recommend not cutting all the wool at once; it is prone to tangle into worms. However, if you are using a mix of colors for the cats or the backgrounds, remember to cut some of each shade or piece of wool and use the strips randomly as you hook to achieve a great texture in your rug.

Making the Rug

1. Transfer the design onto your backing fabric, using the pattern (which needs to be enlarged 500%) on page 43. For details on transferring patterns, see page 132 in "Rug-Hooking Basics." Then either serge or zigzag around the edges by machine or encase the edges in masking tape to prevent raveling as you hook the rug.

2. Begin by hooking the outline of the cats and then filling in the bodies. I hooked my cats by following the shape of the outline and working toward the center. I usually wait until last to hook the eyes and mouth so that I can pick one of the other colors used in the rug. It's easier to decide which color works best after all the colors of the rug have been added. In this case, I ended up using the brown-black background wool for my cats' eyes.

3. Hook the background around the cats. I used an antique brown-black mixture and started by hooking around the cats a couple of times before hooking the border edge. To complete the background, fill in the areas between the background edges and the cats using a swirl-type design rather than straight lines.

4. Hook the colorful triangle points last. I used assorted shades of red, blue, green, gold, and beige to really stand out against the dark background. Hook the perimeter of the triangle first, and then fill in the shape.

Prairie Point Edges

Now for the fun part! I always find that one feature of a rug is more enjoyable to work on than the rest. For this rug, it was the prairie points. I've never made a rug with triangle points around the edge, but I thought it would be fun to try this edge treatment to coordinate with Laurie's "Folky Animals Quilt." After working with the large areas of blue and brown-black, I enjoyed choosing the assorted colors for the points, and they were fun to hook. Although I started with more exaggerated points, I was worried that they might flop over if the rug were hung on a wall. So I shortened the points to 4" across and only 2" deep, and I like the result. Finishing the pointed edge of the rug is a little more challenging, but see "Facing" on page 139 for instructions on finishing a rug like this.

Finishing the Rug

1. Finish your rug using binding tape or fabric. (For tips on tape application and other finishing options, see "Finishing Your Rug" on page 138.) Another option is to finish off the unusual pointed border with a facing. You'll find instructions for that technique on page 139.

2. Steam and block your rug, referring to "Blocking" on page 139.

3. Sew on an identification tag, referring to "Signing Your Rug" on page 140 for various options.

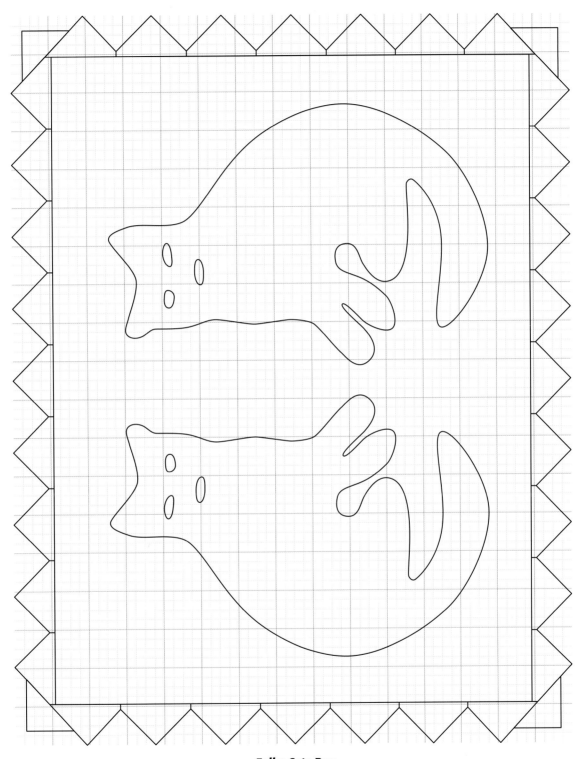

Folky Cats Rug
38" x 30"
1 square = ½"
Enlarge pattern 500%.

Rustic Cabins

How can you think of quilts without thinking of a Log Cabin? Laurie had an idea to do her quilt for some time. When she finished it, she sent me a photo and I decided this was another great project calling out for an accompanying rug. This is my take on the age-old and much-loved Log Cabin pattern.

≈ Polly Minick ≈

No two cabins will ever look alike! This no-pattern technique is guaranteed to give you a folky look. Hand quilted with a large stitch, it will be done in short order.

≈ Laurie Simpson ≈

44

Finished Quilt Size: 80" x 80"
Finished Block Sizes:
Pieced Log Cabins, 8" x 8" • Appliquéd Cabins, 14" x 20"

Log Cabin Quilt

Materials

Yardages are based on 42"-wide fabric.

• 4 yards total of assorted black prints and plaids for pieced Log Cabin blocks, sashing, border corners, and binding

• 3½ yards total of assorted red prints and plaids for pieced Log Cabin blocks and sashing

• 6 fat quarters of black prints for backgrounds of appliquéd blocks

• 6 fat quarters of light plaids, checks, or prints for the "chinking" of appliquéd cabins

• 6 fat quarters of assorted prints or plaids for the appliquéd logs

• 6 assorted scraps, 10" x 10", for cabin roofs

• Assorted light and dark scraps for windows, doors, chimneys, and birds

• 6 yards of backing fabric

• 84" x 84" piece of batting

47

Cutting

All measurements include ¼"-wide seam allowances.

From the assorted black prints and plaids, cut:
• 60 strips, 1½" x 42"; crosscut each strip into the following lengths: 8½", 7½", 6½", 5½", 4½", 3½", 2½", 1½" (Stack a few strips together to make quick work of the cutting.)
• 4 squares, 8½" x 8½"
• 9 binding strips, 2¼" x 42"

From the assorted red prints and plaids, cut:
• 60 strips, 1½" x 42"; crosscut each strip into the following lengths: 7½", 6½", 5½", 4½", 3½", 2½", 1½"

Making the Appliquéd Cabin Blocks

These log cabins are fun, and they give you the freedom to create with no patterns or fussy measurements.

1. Select a black print fat quarter for the background of your first block and press.
2. Select a light fat quarter for the "chinking." From this fabric, cut a rectangle. The size of your rectangle will determine the height and width of your cabin. Notice in the quilt shown that some cabins are taller or wider than others. Each one is unique, but roughly, the dimensions range from 9" to 10½" tall by 11" to 12½" wide. Cut off the top right and left corners of this rectangle to shape the roof of your log cabin.

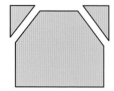

3. Center this piece on the background fabric and machine stitch it in place, sewing ⅛" from the raw edge of the chinking fabric. Turn the piece over and cut away the background fabric that is behind the chinking. Press.

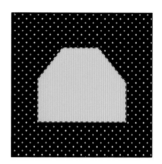

Prints versus Plaids

Woven fabrics work well for the "logs" of the cabin. A print may be used, but the printed design may become distorted along the torn edge. This edge will be finished with needle-turn appliqué, but some of the distortion might still show. If a "rustic" look doesn't bother you, go ahead and use printed fabrics for the logs. Otherwise select woven plaids and checks for your logs, because these fabrics will not distort in this way.

4. Select one of the fat quarters for the appliquéd logs. Tear the fabric into strips varying in width from approximately 1" to 1½". Don't measure—just judge the width by eye. Make a snip at one end of the fabric and rip. Depending on the size of your cabin and the width of your strips, you will need approximately 6 to 10 torn strips. Press these strips.

5. Lay the first log at the bottom of your cabin covering the raw edge of the chinking fabric. The right and left ends of the log should just extend to the sides of the chinking. All of these raw edges will be covered later. Appliqué the top and bottom edges of the first log, turning under the edges as you go. Because the fabric is torn, the edges of the fabric won't necessarily turn under in a uniform way; it tends to act like bias. The appliqué edge will be a little uneven and primitive looking—just like a real log cabin!

6. Place the second log above the first, with the bottom edge just overlapping the top edge of the preceding log. Once the edge is appliquéd there will be a space between the logs where the chinking fabric shows through.

7. Continue adding logs in this manner until your cabin somewhat resembles the following illustration. Leave the roof area bare.

8. To make the roof, tear the roof fabric into strips approximately 1½" wide. (Again, don't measure—tear by eye.) Place the first roof strip at the bottom of the roof area. Overlap the bottom edge as you did for the logs of the cabin walls. Butt the raw ends of the roof "logs" to the ends of the cabin "logs," but do not overlap. These raw edges will be covered later.

9. Appliqué only the bottom edge of each roof log; leave the top edge free. Leave the sides of the roof logs free as you did with the cabin logs. Continue adding roof logs in this manner until you reach the top of the cabin. Appliqué the bottom edge over the preceding log and leave the top edge unsewn.

10. Using the assorted light and dark scraps, cut rectangles for the door, two windows, and chimney, and appliqué in place. Again, judge the size by eye and cut the shapes freehand. Notice in the quilt shown that some doors and windows are wider than others. The chimneys vary in size, too, from short and squat to tall and skinny.

11. Using the strips from your log fabric, appliqué three logs along the roof eaves to cover the raw edges of the logs. Next, appliqué three logs along the vertical edges of the cabin to cover the raw edges of the logs underneath. Lastly, appliqué a log along the top of the roof line, covering the raw edges.

12. To personalize your block, add any appliqué additions you would like to your cabin—birds, animals, trees, or people. Try cutting out these shapes freehand with scissors rather than drawing them first on a pattern. You will be surprised at how well this achieves the "primitive" look.

13. Repeat to make a total of six appliquéd cabin blocks. Set them aside.

Making the Pieced Log Cabin Blocks

When making the Log Cabin blocks, it is most efficient to repeat each step 60 times and then go on to the next step. For instance, use your sewing machine to chain-piece a 1½" black square to a 1½" red square 60 times. Then cut these segments apart and press them open so that you can add the 1½" x 2½" black pieces to them. Continue making the pieced Log Cabin blocks in this manner.

1. Sew the 1½" black squares to the 1½" red squares. Press the seam allowances toward the black fabric.

2. Sew the 2½"-long black strips to the units from step 1. Press the seam allowances toward the newly added strips. As new rounds are sewn, always press the seam allowances in the direction of the newest piece added.

3. Sew the 2½"-long red strips to the units from step 2. Press the units. Turn the units a quarter turn and add the 3½"-long red strips to the next side.

4. Sew the 3½"-long black strips to the units, followed by the 3½"-long red strips. Continue adding the strips in the same manner, with red strips on two adjacent sides of the units and black strips on the other two sides, until all lengths of strips have been added. Note that you will end by adding the final two black strips so each block has seven red pieces and eight black pieces. Your finished blocks should measure 8½" x 8½". Set the blocks aside.

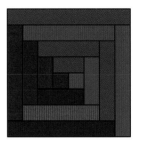

Log Cabin Block
Make 60.

Assembling the Quilt Top

This stage of the quiltmaking is less structured. In fact, it's pretty much free-form. You want to end up with three separate panels, each 48½" long. The two panels of appliquéd cabin blocks should measure 21½" wide, and the center strip of fabric should measure 6½" wide. How you achieve these measurements is up to you! Basic guidelines are given below for achieving the look of the quilt shown, but you can piece yours together however you desire as long as the overall dimensions of the strips equal those given here—otherwise your pieced Log Cabin border blocks will not fit properly around the quilt center.

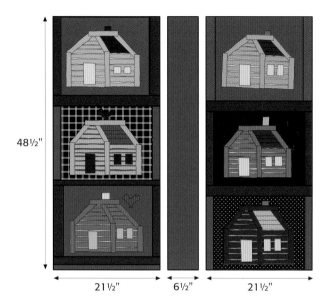

1. The center section is a single piece of black print or plaid fabric cut 6½" x 48½". However, you could piece this section from more than one fabric as long as you end up with this final measurement.

2. For the appliquéd block panels, first trim each block into a rectangle. The blocks shown vary from 17" to 19" wide and 13" to 14" tall. I did the trimming by eye and tried to center the log cabin within each block. Leave enough room around each cabin to have seam allowances for the addition of more fabric.

3. Using the leftover black and red fabrics, cut sashing strips for the blocks. Sashing can be anywhere from 1" to 1¾" finished width. Sew these strips to the blocks so that each block is at least 22½" wide

and at least 17" tall. If they are larger, the excess can easily be trimmed later. Note that in the quilt shown, some of the blocks have sashing strips added only to the sides and not to the top and bottom.

Add sashing to make blocks at least 22½" x 17".

4. Compare the size of your appliquéd blocks. If they vary much in width at this point, add fabric to the narrowest block to bring it closer in size to the others. Press.

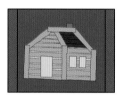

5. Arrange the blocks in two vertical columns of three blocks each. When you're happy with the arrangement, sew the blocks together to make the two panels. Press. Trim each panel to exactly 48½" long and 21½" wide. If your panels are still too small, add fabric to the entire length or width until they are large enough.

6. Sew the two appliquéd panels to either side of the plain panel. At this point your quilt top should measure exactly 48½" x 48½" square so that the pieced Log Cabin block border will fit accurately.

7. Lay out the Log Cabin blocks using the photograph on page 46 as a guide. Make sure your blocks are oriented correctly so that they form a red zigzag frame around the quilt center. The 8½" black squares form the four border corners.

8. Piece together the Log Cabin blocks into sections as shown. Press. Sew the two side border sections to the sides of the quilt center. Press the seam allowances toward the quilt center. Then sew the top and bottom border sections to the quilt and press in the same fashion.

Quilt Assembly

Finishing the Quilt

1. Choose a quilting design, and then follow the directions for marking the quilt top as described in "Quiltmaking Basics" on page 124.

2. From the backing fabric, cut two pieces, 88" long. Remove the selvages and join the pieces to make an 83½" x 88" backing piece. Press the seam open.

3. Center and layer the quilt top and batting over the backing; baste the layers together, and then quilt as desired. The quilt shown was hand quilted in an allover Baptist fan pattern using a large quilting stitch, which is a great way of hand quilting a top that has lots of seams.

4. Trim the batting and backing even with the edges of the quilt top. Use the 2¼" x 42" black strips to bind the quilt, referring to page 124 in "Quiltmaking Basics" as needed.

5. Make a label and attach it to the back of your quilt.

Finished Rug Size: 48" x 40"

Log Cabin Rug
with Quilt-Block Border

Materials

Wool yardages are estimated based on 60"-wide fabric. (See "How Much Wool Do You Need?" on page 133 for more information on estimating yardage before beginning any project.)

• 3 yards total of dark brown and black check, tweed, and plaid wools for background, roof, and border

• 2½ yards total of assorted red wools for chimney and border

• 1¼ yards total of assorted bright blue wools for cabin walls

• ½ yard of mustard wool for door, windows, and chinking

• ¼ yard of darker bright blue wool for edge of cabin

• 58" x 47" piece of backing fabric*

• 200" of binding tape

*If you use a hoop, add 8" to the background measurements. See "Rug Backing" on page 132 for more information on fabric-measuring techniques and backing options.

Cutting

Cut your wool into size #8 or #9 strips, referring to "Cutting the Strips" on page 133. I recommend not cutting all the wool at once; it is prone to tangle into worms.

However, if you are using a combination of shades for one area, such as the mixture of brown and black used in the background, remember to cut some of each piece to hook with for a great textured look.

Making the Rug

1. Transfer the design onto your backing fabric, using the pattern (which needs to be enlarged 600%) on page 57. For details on transferring patterns, see page 132 in "Rug-Hooking Basics." Then either serge or zigzag around the edges by machine or encase the edges in masking tape to prevent raveling as you hook the rug.

2. Hook the outline of the cabin using the darker bright blue wool, and then fill in the cabin walls, door, windows, and roof. It will be easier to hook straight lines for the chinking if you hook those single rows of loops first with the mustard wool, and then fill in the lighter bright blue between them.

3. Hook the roof in the same manner, using single rows of brown loops first and then filling in the spaces between them with rows of dark red loops. Use dark red to hook the chimney too.

4. Fill in the background with your brown and black wool mixture to finish the center of the rug.

5. The Log Cabin–style border is both fun and challenging. Use any number of colors in the blocks; I used as many dark brown and black wools as I could to coordinate with the background, and as many reds as I could find that coordinated well with the roof. Refer to the project photograph for color placement.

Finishing the Rug

1. Finish your rug using binding tape. (For tips on tape application and other finishing options, see "Finishing Your Rug" on page 138.)

2. Steam and block your rug, referring to "Blocking" on page 139.

3. Sew on an identification tag, referring to "Signing Your Rug" on page 140 for various options.

Log Cabin Rug with Quilt-Block Border
48" x 40"
1 square = ½"
Enlarge pattern 600%.

Anchors Aweigh

A vintage U.S. Navy blanket circa WWII was the
starting point for this penny rug. Military blankets
can be found at flea markets and at online auctions.
This project is a great way to use a blanket that may have
some moth damage. Always wash vintage wool
before adding it to your fabric collection.

❧ *Laurie Simpson* ☙

I am always inclined to work on patriotic pieces,
as I do love to make and display them. This time
I decided to go with a "shape" rug, making my
red-white-and-blue project in the form of the shield
that Laurie used on her beautiful penny rug.

❧ *Polly Minick* ☙

Finished Rug Size: 23" x 46"

Sailor Penny Rug

Materials

• 40" x 48" piece of off-white wool or a vintage U.S. Navy wool blanket

• Wool scraps in the following colors: black, dark blue, light blue, flesh tone, gold, red

• Needlepoint wool or pearl cotton in the following colors and amounts: 5 skeins of navy blue; 3 skeins of gray; 4 skeins of red; 1 skein each of off-white, gold, and flesh tone

• ⅝ yard of cotton fabric for backing

Cutting

The appliqué patterns are on pages 64–67. Do not add seam allowances for wool appliqué.

From the red wool, cut:
   • 54 stars
   • 1 shield

From the off-white wool or blanket, cut:
   • 1 background rectangle, 17" x 40"
(Note: If you are using a Navy blanket, cut the fabric so that the words are centered across the 17" width and begin approxi-

mately 8" from the bottom of the rectangle.)
- 54 tongues
- 4 stripes for shield

From the dark blue wool, cut:
- 1 shield top
- 2 anchors
- 1 hat bottom
- 1 hat top
- 1 neckerchief
- 1 pair of bell bottoms

From the light blue wool, cut:
- 1 shirt

From the black wool, cut:
- Shoes

From the flesh-tone wool, cut:
- Face and hands

From the gold wool, cut:
- 1 oar

From the cotton backing fabric, cut:
- 1 piece, 18" x 41"

Easy Wool Marking

If you can't find a U.S. Navy blanket and want to duplicate the letters on plain wool, you can use a simple stencil to trace and cut letters from navy wool and blanket stitch them in place. The letters on the blanket shown are about 2" high.

Another way to create the letters is to print them out on your computer in a large font size and trace them onto freezer paper to make patterns for cutting the letters out of wool.

Appliquéing the Penny Rug

1. Using a sharp embroidery or chenille needle and one strand of red needle-point wool or pearl cotton, appliqué a red star onto each tongue using the blanket stitch. Blanket stitch around the edge of each tongue using navy needlepoint wool. Set aside.

2. Appliqué the four white stripes onto the red shield using off-white needlepoint wool. Position the shield at the upper end of the 17" x 40" background so that the top points of the shield are about 4" from the top edge of the background and the shield is centered from side to side. Appliqué in place using navy needlepoint wool.

3. Appliqué the dark blue shield top in place using off-white needlepoint wool. Embroider off-white stars onto the shield top, referring to the photograph on page 60 for placement.

Bring needle up at 1 and down at 2.

Bring needle up at 3 and down at 2.

Bring needle up at 4 and down at 2, up at 5 and down at 2, up at 6 and down at 2.

62

4. Using the blanket stitch, appliqué the sailor and anchors in the following order: shirt (leave cuffs open for hands), shoes, bell bottoms, face and neck, neckerchief, oar, hat bottom, hat top, hands, anchors. I used gray needlepoint wool for all the clothing, gold for the oar, flesh tone for the hands and face, and navy blue for the anchors.

Finishing the Rug

1. By eye, arrange the tongues around the penny rug; there's no need to measure. Pin them in place with the tongues extending by about ½" to the back of the rug. Whipstitch the flat edge of the tongues onto the back of the penny rug, taking care not to sew through to the front.

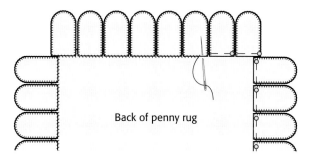

Back of penny rug

2. Using navy blue needlepoint wool, blanket stitch around the perimeter of the penny rug, catching the top of each tongue as you go.

3. Pin the piece of backing fabric, right side up, onto the back of the penny rug. Turn under the raw edges of the cotton backing so that the cotton fabric is the same size as the wool rug. Blindstitch in place by hand.

4. Make a label and attach it to the back of your penny rug.

Do not add seam allowances
for wool appliqué.

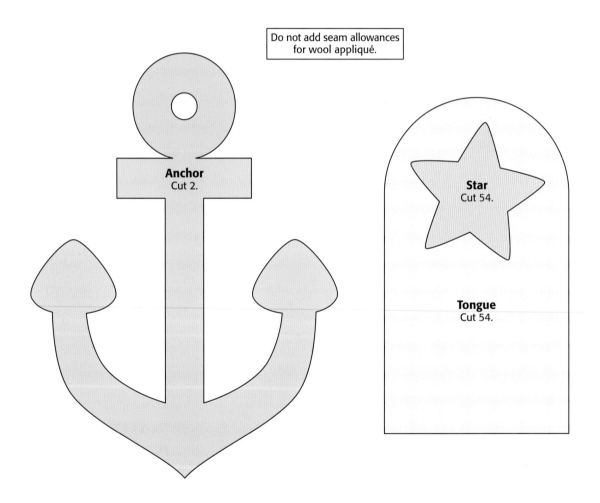

Anchor
Cut 2.

Star
Cut 54.

Tongue
Cut 54.

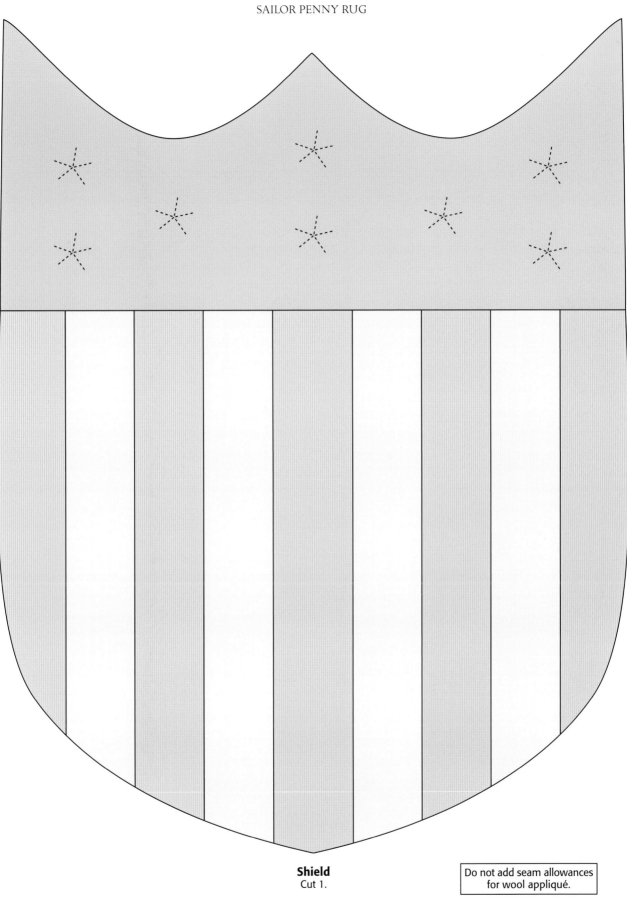

Shield
Cut 1.

Do not add seam allowances
for wool appliqué.

Do not add seam allowances
for wool appliqué.

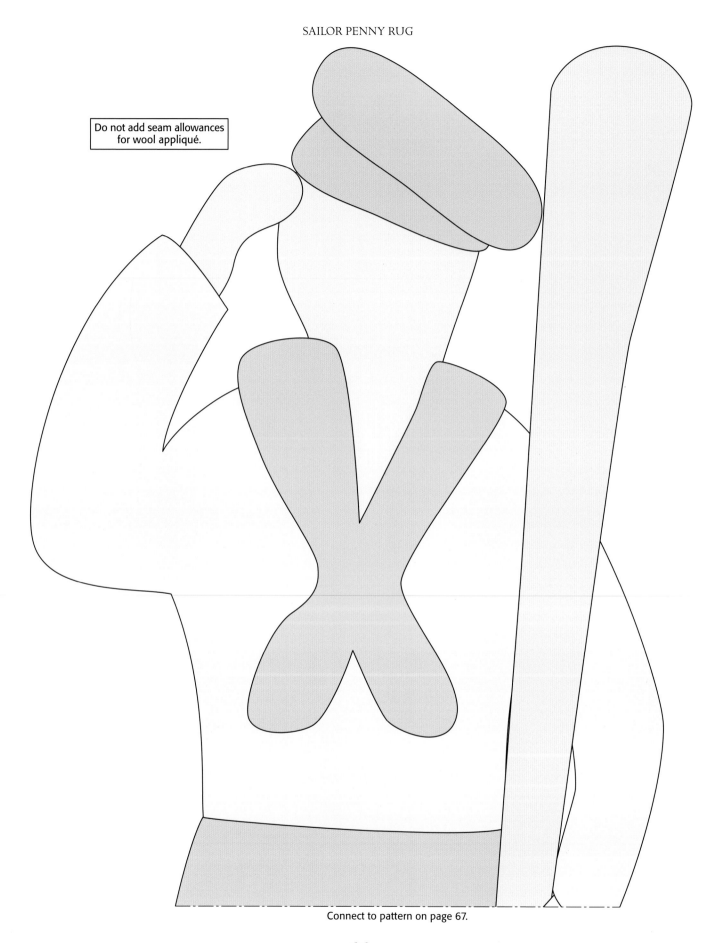

Connect to pattern on page 67.

Connect to pattern on page 66.

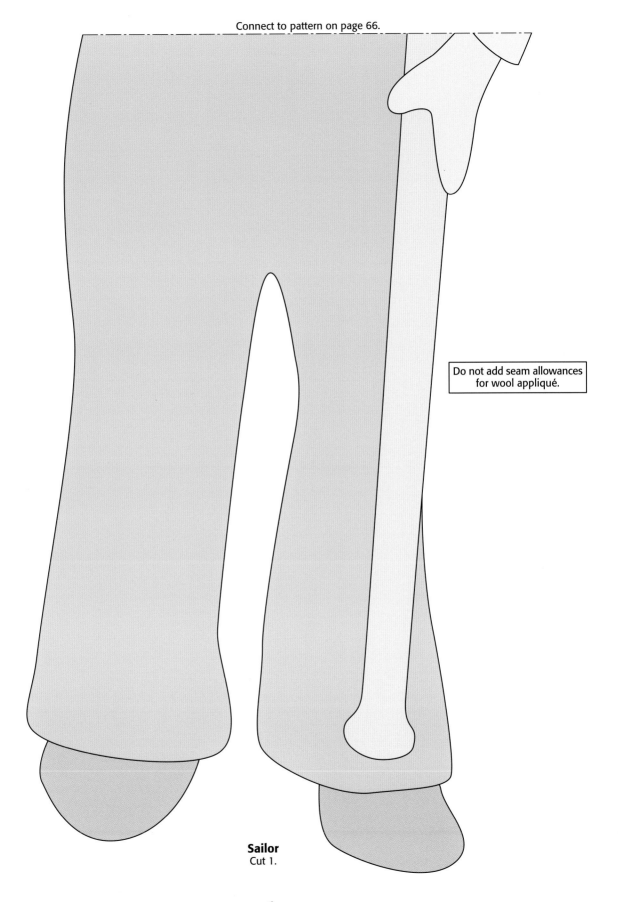

Do not add seam allowances
for wool appliqué.

Sailor
Cut 1.

Finished Rug Size: 30" x 38"

Patriotic Shield Rug

Materials

Wool yardages are estimated based on 60"-wide fabric. (See "How Much Wool Do You Need?" on page 133 for more information on estimating yardage before beginning any project.)

• 1½ yards total of assorted off-white wools for stars and stripes

• 1 yard total of assorted red wools for stripes

• ½ yard total of assorted navy and indigo blue wools for star field

• 38" x 46" piece of backing fabric*

• 175" of binding tape *or* ⅜ yard of striped fabric as used in this rug for a facing

*If you use a hoop, add 8" to the background measurements. See "Rug Backing" on page 132 for more information on fabric-measuring techniques and backing options.

Cutting

Cut your wool into size #8 or #9 strips, referring to "Cutting the Strips" on page 133. I recommend not cutting all the wool at once; it is prone to tangle into worms. However, be sure to cut some strips of each of the various reds, off-whites, and blues so that as you hook, you can mix them up for better texture.

Making the Rug

1. Transfer the design onto your backing fabric, using the pattern (which needs to be enlarged 400%) on page 71. For details on transferring patterns, see page 132 in "Rug-Hooking Basics." Then either serge or zigzag around the edges by machine or encase the edges in masking tape to prevent raveling as you hook the rug.

2. Hook the stars, outlining them first and then filling them in using a mixture of the off-white strips.

3. Using a variety of navy and indigo blues, hook the field behind the stars.

4. Hook the stripes in vertical rows, making sure you are using a mixture of the reds and off-whites.

Finishing the Rug

1. Finish your rug using binding tape, or you may choose vintage fabric as I used on this rug. Because binding tape is not stretchy, you might find it difficult to maneuver the tape around the curved portions of this rug. To use fabric, I recommend making a facing as I did on the rug shown. This works more effectively on the shield shape than cutting the fabric into strips and trying to use the strips in the same manner as binding tape. For tips on tape application and other finishing options such as making a facing, see "Finishing Your Rug" on page 138.

2. Steam and block your rug, referring to "Blocking" on page 139.

3. Sew on an identification tag, referring to "Signing Your Rug" on page 140 for various options.

An antique corner shelf is home to Polly's collection of sand pails from the early 1900s, right.

Below, several more patriotic sand pails decorate a splay-legged table with a red-and-white painted checkerboard top.

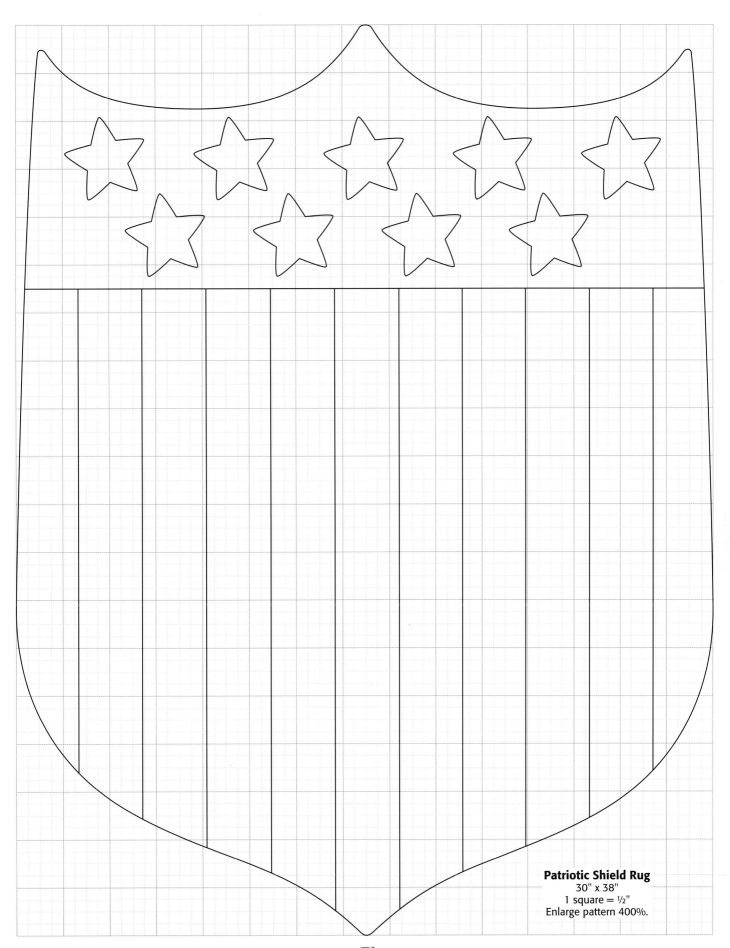

Patriotic Shield Rug
30" x 38"
1 square = ¹⁄₂"
Enlarge pattern 400%.

Irish Chain

Indigos and white are a timeless combination. Lots of scraps in many values are used to give dimension to the village figures. My husband, Bill, who is an ice hockey coach, was the inspiration for this quilt.

Laurie Simpson

Working on this book with Laurie got me to look seriously at quilt patterns that intrigue me. I have always been a fan of the Irish Chain, and after Laurie stitched the Snow Day quilt, I decided to make a rug using only two colors. While two-color rugs are not common, I not only enjoyed the challenge, but I was also thrilled with the outcome.

Polly Minick

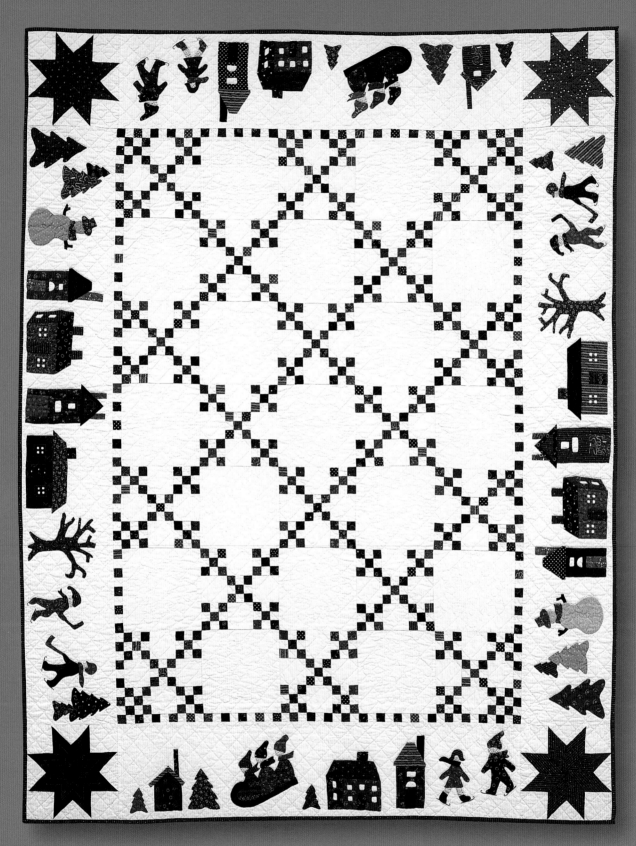

Finished Quilt Size: 67½" x 85½"
Finished Block Size: 9"

Snow Day Quilt

Materials

Yardages are based on 42"-wide fabric.

• 5 yards of solid white fabric

• 3½ yards total of assorted indigo fabrics

• 1 skein of indigo embroidery floss

• 5¼ yards of backing fabric

• 70" x 90" piece of batting

Cutting

All measurements include ¼"-wide seam allowances. The diamond pattern is on page 79.

From the indigo fabrics, cut:
    • 560 squares, 1½" x 1½"
    • 32 diamonds
    • 8 binding strips, 2¼" x 42"
    • Save all the indigo scraps for the appliqué border.

From the white fabric, cut on the lengthwise grain:
    • 2 border strips, 10½" x 67"
    • 2 border strips, 10½" x 49"

From the remaining white fabric, cut:
    • 17 squares, 9½" x 9½"
    • 88 squares, 3½" x 3½"
    • 470 squares, 1½" x 1½"
    • 4 squares, 5½" x 5½"; cut each square in half twice diagonally to yield a total of 16 triangles

Making the Double Nine Patch Blocks

1. Select five assorted 1½" indigo squares and four 1½" white squares. Sew the squares together into rows, and then sew the rows together to make a small Nine Patch block. Your blocks should

measure 3½" x 3½" including the outside seam allowances. Repeat to make a total of 90 small Nine Patches. Press.

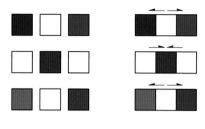

Make 90.

2. Lay out five of the small Nine Patch blocks and four 3½" white squares as shown. Sew the units together into rows, and then sew the rows together

to make a Double Nine Patch block (also known as Single Irish Chain blocks). Repeat to make a total of 18 blocks. (Note: You will have leftover 3½" white squares; reserve them for the LeMoyne Star blocks in the border.) If you are hand piecing, press the seam intersections in the same manner described in "Clever Pressing" below.

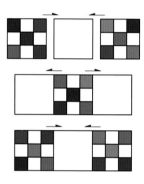

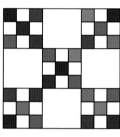

Double Nine Patch
Make 18.

Clever Pressing

I pieced my quilt by hand, and when doing so, I don't sew across any of the seam allowances. The beauty of this is that I am free to press seams in any direction. For a Nine Patch, I like to press the seams so that from the wrong side the intersections form tiny four-patch designs. The reason I press this way is to distribute the bulk, thus making my blocks lie flatter and the finished block easier to quilt.

When these nine-patch sections are hand pieced they should be pressed as shown below. If you'd like to press machine-pieced blocks in this manner, you'll need to either clip away some of the stitching or clip through the seam allowance itself. This will weaken the seam intersection, so you may need to just press traditionally and live with extra bulk at the seam intersections.

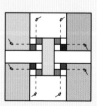

Assembling the Quilt Top

1. Lay out the patchwork blocks with the 9½" white squares as shown in the diagram to form the Irish Chain pattern. Sew the blocks together into rows, and then sew the rows together. Press.

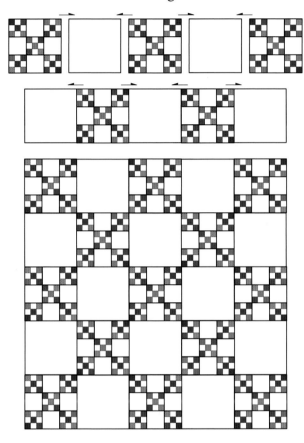

2. Sew together 32 of the 1½" white squares and 31 of the 1½" indigo squares into a strip, starting and ending with a white square. Repeat. Sew these strips to the sides of the quilt top. Press the seam allowances toward the outside.

3. Sew together 24 of the 1½" indigo squares and 23 of the 1½" white squares into a strip, starting and ending with an indigo square. Repeat. Sew these strips to the top and bottom of the quilt top. Press the seam allowances toward the outside.

Making the Appliqué Border

1. Enlarge the patterns on pages 80–83 160% and then prepare the appliqués. In the quilt shown, the side borders are the same and the top and bottom borders are the same. The side borders each use houses 1–4; a snowman; two hockey players; two small, two medium, and one large evergreen tree; and one bare-branched tree.

   The top and bottom borders each use houses 1, 5, and 6; two small and one medium evergreen tree; a boy and a girl ice skater; and three children on a toboggan.

2. Arranging by eye, lay out the appliqués for the side borders on the two 10½" x 67" white strips and follow the appliqué directions on pages 119–121 in "Quiltmaking Basics." Press.

3. Trim the side borders to a length of 65¼". Attach them to the left and right sides of the quilt, orienting the strips so that the figures face toward the outside. Press the seam allowances toward the appliqué borders.

4. Arrange the appliqués for the top and bottom borders on the two 10½" x 49" white strips, and then appliqué the pieces in place. Press. Trim the borders to a length of 47½" and set them aside.

5. Piece the LeMoyne Star blocks for the

border corners. First, sew the indigo diamonds together in pairs, and then sew the pairs together. Join the two halves of the star points.

6. Using the remaining 3½" white squares and the triangles cut from the 5½" white squares, set in the corner squares and the side triangles on the blocks. For setting in the seams, see steps 6–8 of "Making the LeMoyne Star Blocks" on pages 13 and 14.

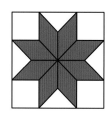

LeMoyne Star
Make 4.

7. Sew a LeMoyne Star block to each end of the 10½" x 47½" borders. Press the seam allowances toward the border strips. Attach the borders to the top and bottom of the quilt, and press the seam allowances toward the appliqué borders.

Press for Success

Press the LeMoyne Star block pieces after the entire block is pieced. Press the seam allowances all in one direction.

Embroidered sheets are perfect accompaniments for antiques.

Finishing the Quilt

1. Choose a quilting design and then follow the directions for marking the quilt top as described in "Quiltmaking Basics" on page 123.

2. From the backing fabric, cut two pieces, 91" long. Remove the selvages and join the pieces. Trim to make a 72" x 91" backing piece. Press the seam open.

3. Center and layer the quilt top and batting over the backing; baste the layers together, and then quilt as desired. The quilt shown was hand quilted with a snowflake motif in the center of each large white square. The Double Nine Patch blocks were quilted with diagonal lines in one direction only, while the appliquéd borders were quilted diagonally in both directions for crosshatching.

4. Trim the batting and backing even with the edges of the quilt top. Use the 2¼" x 42" indigo strips to bind the quilt.

5. Make a label and attach it to the back of your quilt.

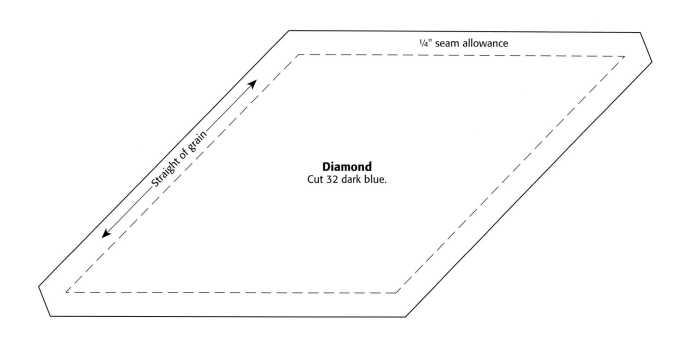

¼" seam allowance

Straight of grain

Diamond
Cut 32 dark blue.

Hockey Player 1
Cut 2.

Bare-Branched Tree
Cut 2.

Enlarge patterns 160%.
Add ¼" seam allowances
for hand appliqué.

Snowman
Cut 2.

Hockey Player 2
Cut 2.

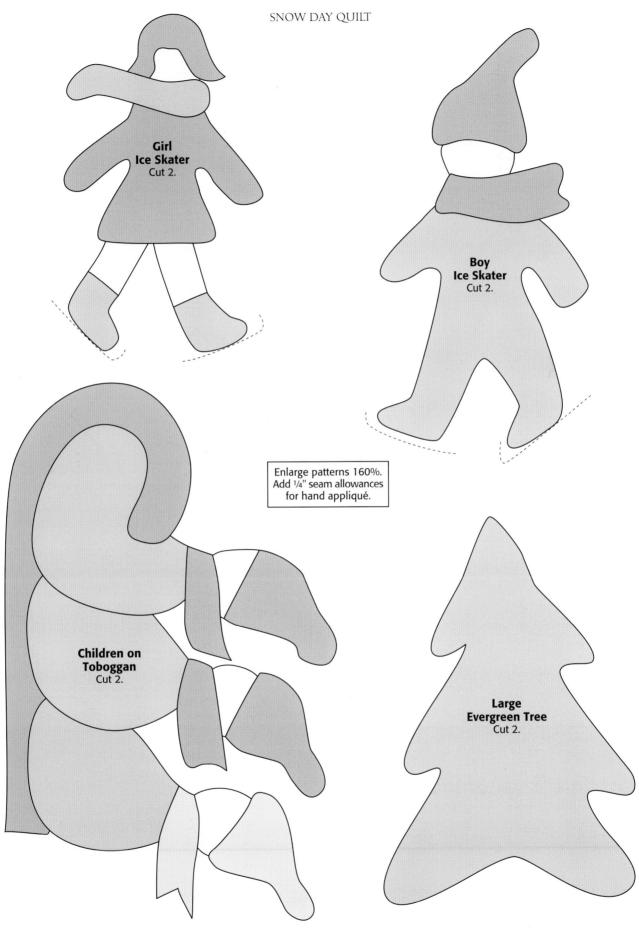

**Girl
Ice Skater**
Cut 2.

**Boy
Ice Skater**
Cut 2.

Enlarge patterns 160%.
Add ¼" seam allowances
for hand appliqué.

**Children on
Toboggan**
Cut 2.

**Large
Evergreen Tree**
Cut 2.

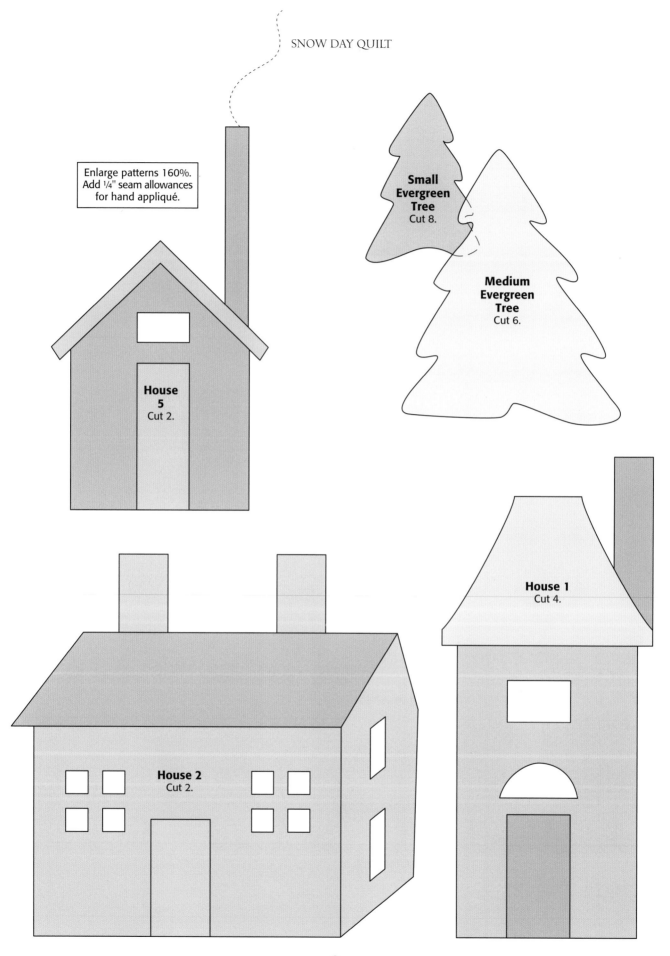

Enlarge patterns 160%.
Add 1/4" seam allowances
for hand appliqué.

Small
Evergreen
Tree
Cut 8.

Medium
Evergreen
Tree
Cut 6.

House
5
Cut 2.

House 1
Cut 4.

House 2
Cut 2.

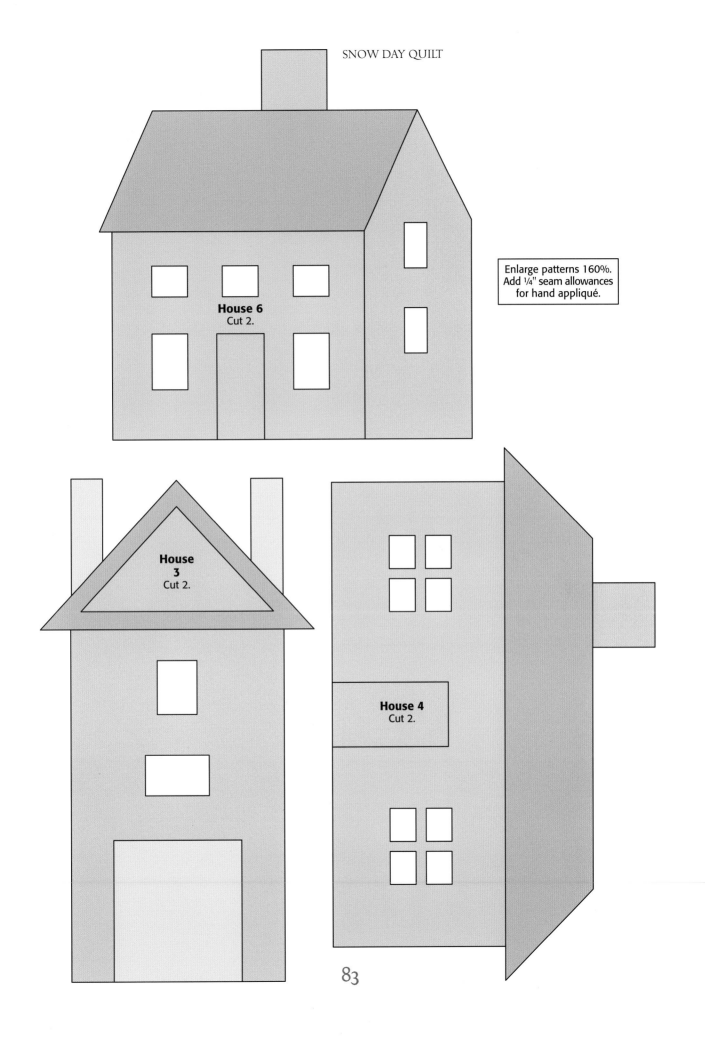

Enlarge patterns 160%.
Add ¼" seam allowances
for hand appliqué.

House 6
Cut 2.

**House
3**
Cut 2.

House 4
Cut 2.

Finished Rug Size: 36" x 45"

Irish Chain Rug

Materials

Wool yardages are estimated based on 60"-wide fabric. (See "How Much Wool Do You Need?" on page 133 for more information on estimating yardage before beginning any project.)

• 2½ to 3 yards total of assorted off-white wools for background

• 2 yards total of many assorted blue wools for Irish Chain

• ¼ yard each of 6 coordinating blue wools for large stars

• 43" x 52" piece of backing fabric*

• 185" of binding tape *or* ¾ yard of vintage ticking fabric as used on this rug

*If you use a hoop, add 8" to the background measurements. See "Rug Backing" on page 132 for more information on fabric-measuring techniques and backing options.

Cutting

Cut your wool into size #8 or #9 strips, referring to "Cutting the Strips" on page 133. I recommend not cutting all the wool at once; it is prone to tangle into worms. However, be sure to cut some strips of each of the various whites for the background hooking.

Making the Rug

1. Transfer the design onto your backing fabric, using the pattern (which needs to be enlarged 500%) on page 87. For details on transferring patterns, see page 132 in "Rug-Hooking Basics." Then either serge or zigzag around the edges by machine or encase the edges in masking tape to prevent raveling as you hook the rug.

2. Hook the stars first. Outline each star point individually and then fill in the diamonds.

3. After you have hooked the six stars, hook the off-white backgrounds of the stars. Rather than hooking the entire background area as a single unit, I wanted to mimic the look of quilt blocks stitched together. To achieve this, I used a slightly different shade of off-white for each star background. I hooked a square around each star and filled in the squares individually.

4. Notice that the border of this rug, which is hooked in an Irish Chain design, is actually made in a grid of four Double Nine Patch blocks across the top and bottom and five blocks along the sides. I hooked each block in its entirety

before moving on to the next block. Hook all the blues within a block first, and then fill in the off-white areas of that block.

Finishing the Rug

1. Finish your rug using binding tape or vintage ticking as I did for the rug shown. I often use ticking (it's just as sturdy as rug-binding tape) and I particularly like how this blue-and-white rug looks with just a glimpse of the ticking peeking around the edges. (For tips on tape application and other finishing options, see "Finishing Your Rug" on page 138.)

2. Steam and block the rug, referring to "Blocking" on page 139.

3. Sew on an identification tag, referring to "Signing Your Rug" on page 140 for various options.

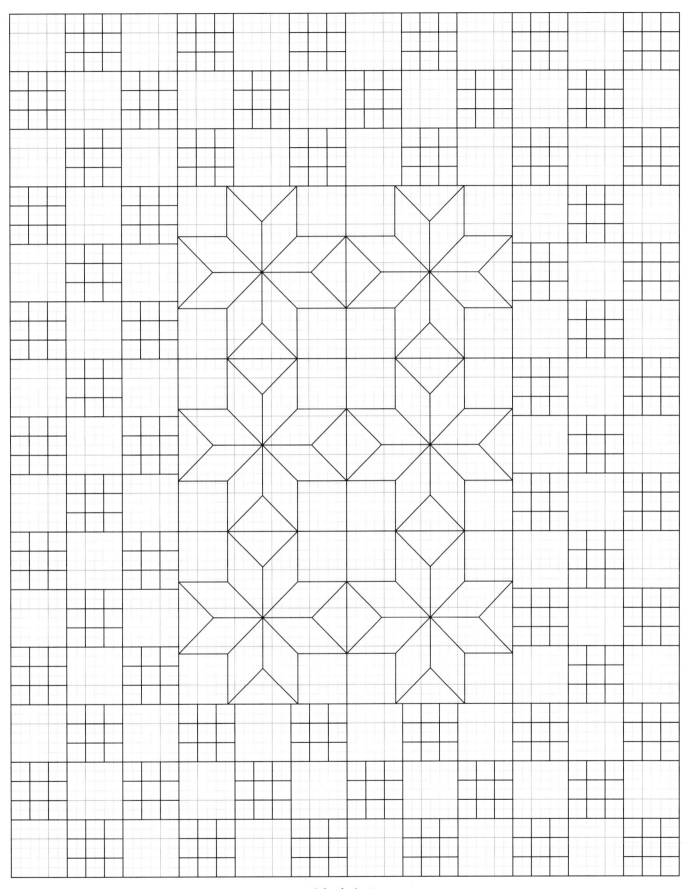

Irish Chain Rug
36" x 45"
1 square = ½"
Enlarge pattern 500%.

Mariner's Compass

Another quilt design, the Mariner's Compass, was the starting point for this nautical-themed rug. Since living along the coast for the past few years, I am drawn more to designing maritime-inspired pieces. This was a fun rug to make for our new home in Naples, Florida. The waves, sailboats, compass, and anchors look right at home in our place near the water.

Polly Minick

Antique wool ticking provided plenty of inspiration for this small quilt. Wool is lovely to work with and quilts like a dream.

Laurie Simpson

Finished Quilt Size: 41½" x 51½"
including prairie points

Nautical Wool Quilt

Materials

• 38" x 48" piece of blue plaid wool for background

• 1 fat quarter each of light gray and 2 different blue-and-white striped wool fabrics for appliqués

• Scraps of dark blue, light blue, gold, off-white, and red wool fabrics for appliqués

• 76 squares, 4" x 4", of cotton fabrics in coordinating colors for prairie points

• 1⅜ yards of 60"-wide cotton fabric (or 1⅝ yards of 42"-wide fabric) for backing

• 42" x 54" piece of batting

• 8 skeins of needlepoint wool in assorted shades of gray

• Spool of linen thread

Cutting

The appliqué patterns are on pages 94–95. They need to be enlarged 200%. Do not add seam allowances for wool appliqué.

From one blue-and-white striped wool, cut:
  • Large sails 1 and 2

From the other blue-and-white striped wool, cut:
  • Small sails 1 and 2

From the light gray striped wool, cut:
  • 1 sand pail exterior
  • 1 shovel
  • 4 large spires

From the off-white wool, cut:
  • 4 medium spires

From the dark blue wool, cut:
  • 8 small spires
  • 1 sand pail interior

From the light blue wool, cut:
- 1 small sailboat hull
- 1 sand pail handle

From the red wool, cut:
- 1 large sailboat hull

From the gold wool, cut:
- 1 mariner's compass center

From the cotton backing fabric, cut:
- 1 piece, 44" x 54"

Appliquéing the Quilt Top

1. Place the appliqué shapes on the blue background wool in a pleasing arrangement. Pin them in place.
2. Using a sharp tapestry or chenille needle and one strand of needlepoint wool, blanket stitch the shapes onto the wool backing in the following order.
   a: Light gray large spires, pointing N, S, E, and W
   b: Off-white medium spires pointing NE, SE, SW, and NW
   c: Dark blue small spires, placed between the preceding spires
   d: Gold center of mariner's compass
   e: Sails of large boat
   f: Hull of large sailboat
   g: Sails of small boat
   h: Hull of small sailboat
   i: Sand pail exterior
   j: Sand pail interior
   k: Sand pail handle (Embroider the wire portion of the pail's handle using one strand of wool and a backstitch or outline stitch.)
   l: Shovel

3. Steam press the quilt top after the addition of each appliquéd piece to make sure that the quilt top lies flat.
4. Press each 4" cotton square in half twice diagonally to make the prairie points.

Prairie Point
Make 76.

5. Lay out the prairie points along each edge of the quilt top, tucking the folded point of each one into the open edge of the prairie point next to it as shown. Adjust the spacing by eye and then pin them into place. I used 17 on the short ends of the quilt and 21 on each long edge. Machine baste the prairie points to the quilt top, sewing a scant $\frac{1}{4}$" from the edge of the quilt top.

Finishing the Quilt

1. Center and layer the quilt top and batting over the backing. Pin baste or thread baste the layers together. Basting spray does not work well with wool.

2. Quilt as desired, but do not quilt the outer ½" along the edges of the quilt. Take care not to quilt through the prairie points—move each one out of your way as you quilt close to it. The quilt shown is quilted with diagonal crosshatching spaced at 2" intervals.

Quick Stitches

You will need to use a much larger needle and quilting stitch on a wool quilt than you would on a cotton quilt, but other than that, the mechanics of the quilting stitch are the same. I used a crewel embroidery needle and took large, even quilting stitches. You'll be surprised at how quickly you can complete this type of quilting.

3. After quilting is complete, *trim only the batting* to the exact size of the finished quilt top (not including the ¼" seam allowance all around). Trim the backing fabric so that it is ½" larger all the way around than the quilt.

4. To finish the edge of the quilt, turn the prairie points up, away from the quilt center. This will turn the outer edge of the quilt top down and around the batting. Fold the top edge of the backing fabric toward the inside of the quilt to cover the raw edge of the batting and the prairie points. All raw edges should be hidden. Pin in place, and then blindstitch around all edges.

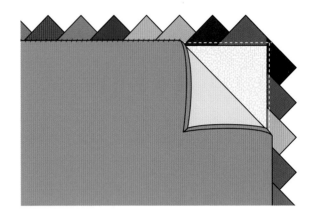

5. Quilt ¼" from the outer edges of the quilt using the linen thread and a long running stitch. This will help hold the edges firmly in place and also form a decorative treatment just inside the prairie points.

Quilt Plan

6. Make a label and attach it to the back of your quilt.

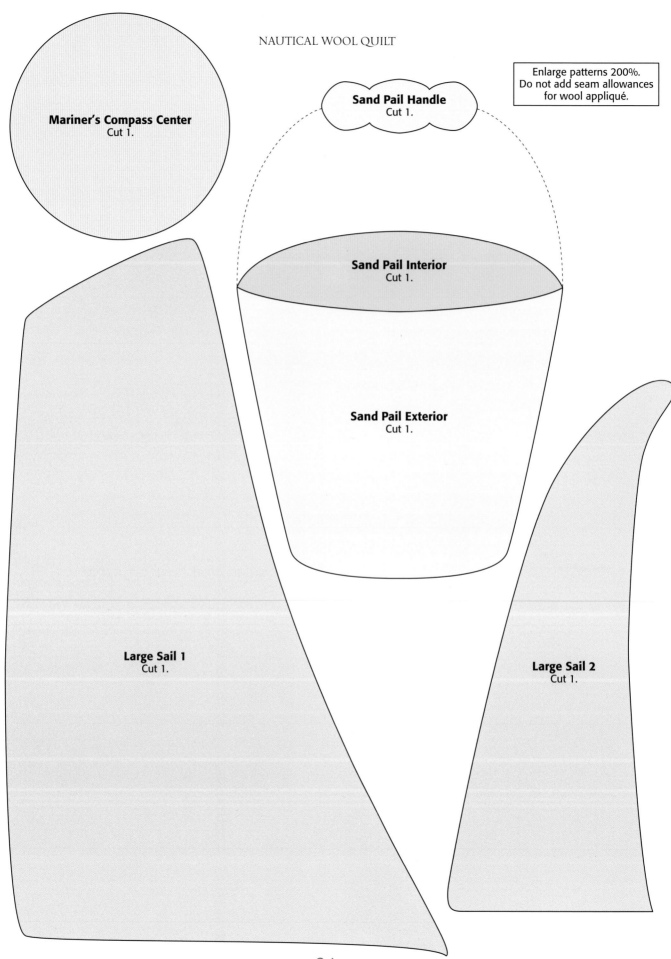

Mariner's Compass Center
Cut 1.

Sand Pail Handle
Cut 1.

Enlarge patterns 200%.
Do not add seam allowances
for wool appliqué.

Sand Pail Interior
Cut 1.

Sand Pail Exterior
Cut 1.

Large Sail 1
Cut 1.

Large Sail 2
Cut 1.

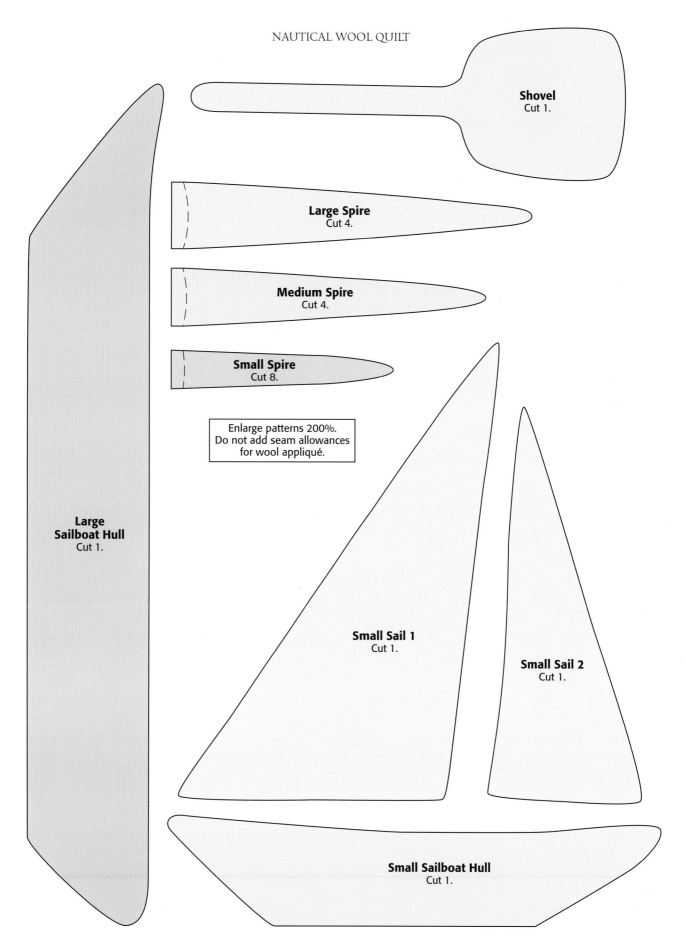

Shovel
Cut 1.

Large Spire
Cut 4.

Medium Spire
Cut 4.

Small Spire
Cut 8.

Enlarge patterns 200%.
Do not add seam allowances
for wool appliqué.

**Large
Sailboat Hull**
Cut 1.

Small Sail 1
Cut 1.

Small Sail 2
Cut 1.

Small Sailboat Hull
Cut 1.

Finished Rug Size: 34" x 23"

Mariner's Compass Rug

Materials

Wool yardages are estimated based on 60"-wide fabric. (See "How Much Wool Do You Need?" on page 133 for more information on estimating yardage before beginning any project.)

• 1¾ yards total of assorted blue wools for background and border

• ¾ yard of gray-and-white checked wool for star points, sailboat hull, and border

• ½ yard total of assorted off-white wools for star, sails, and anchors

• ¼ yard of old red wool for letters, sailboat hull, and flag

• ⅛ yard of gold wool for sailboat hull and flag

• ⅛ yard of beige wool for sailboat hull, star outline, and flag

• 4 to 6 strips of light blue wool for flag

• 4 to 6 strips of black wool for masts

• 55" x 40" piece of backing fabric*

• 165" of binding tape *or* ¼ yard of red-and-white ticking fabric as used on this rug

*If you use a hoop, add 8" to the background measurements. See "Rug Backing" on page 132 for more information on fabric-measuring techniques and backing options.

Cutting

Cut your wool into size #8 or #9 strips, referring to "Cutting the Strips" on page 133. I recommend not cutting all the wool at once; it is prone to tangle into worms. However, if you are using an assortment of blues in the background as I did, make sure you cut some of each shade, mix up the strips, and use them randomly.

Making the Rug

1. Transfer the design onto your backing fabric, using the pattern (which needs to be enlarged 400%) on page 99. For details on transferring patterns, see page 132 in "Rug-Hooking Basics." Then either serge or zigzag around the edges by machine or encase the edges in masking tape to prevent raveling as you hook the rug.
2. Begin hooking in the center of the rug, outlining the star with beige wool and then filling in the shape with off-white. The smaller star points are filled in with the gray-and-white check.

3. Hook the letters and sailboats, using off-white for the sails, red for the letters, black for the masts, and red, gold, beige, and gray-and-white check for the hulls. Mix and match the colors to hook the flags atop the masts.
4. Hook the border and corner blocks next to make a nice straight line for the background's border.
5. Fill in the background, making sure to use a mixture of all your assorted blue wools.

Finishing the Rug

1. Finish your rug using binding tape or ticking fabric as shown here. (For tips on tape application and other finishing options, see "Finishing Your Rug" on page 138.)
2. Steam and block the rug, referring to "Blocking" on page 139.
3. Sew on an identification tag, referring to "Signing Your Rug" on page 140 for various options.

Polly collects both vintage sand pails and sailboats, both of which have inspired rug designs. The rug shown here depicts a variety of her patriotic pails.

Mariner's Compass Rug
34" x 23"
1 square = ½"
Enlarge pattern 400%.

America's Pastime

Our family's love of baseball is the theme of these projects. My large quilt, shown opposite, tells the story of family members who have played, and it conveys my feelings as a fan. I designed the larger quilt in the style of a nineteenth-century album quilt. The smaller quilt pictured here uses some of the same features, such as red-white-and-blue bunting in the border.

❧ Laurie Simpson ❧

After seeing Laurie's wonderful quilt, I wanted my rug to showcase baseball as it relates to our family. All of our sons played the game, two in college and one professionally. And our grandfather played in a league at the turn of the twentieth century. My border features some of the words from "Take Me Out to the Ball Game" by Jack Norworth, in honor of our aunt, who requested that the song be sung at her funeral. So I think you understand the love of baseball in our family! I would also like to thank Frito-Lay for allowing us to use their logo in our work. And now that all three of our grandsons are enjoying "America's Pastime," this project was even more fun and memorable to work on.

❧ Polly Minick ❧

CRACKERJACK is a registered trademark of Frito-Lay North America, Inc., © Frito-Lay North America, Inc., 2004.

Finished Quilt Size: 42½" x 56½" • Finished Block Size: 12"

Baseball Quilt

Materials

Yardages are based on 42"-wide fabric.

• 2 yards of khaki striped fabric for sashing, border, and binding

• 6 fat quarters of assorted tan fabrics for block backgrounds and sashing squares

• 1 yard total of assorted red fabrics for bunting and appliqués

• ½ yard total of assorted blue fabrics for bunting and appliqués

• 1 fat quarter of tan or off-white fabric for bunting and appliqués

• ¼ yard total of assorted gold fabrics for appliqués

• 10" square of brown fabric for appliqués

• 2¾ yards of backing fabric

• 48" x 61" piece of batting

• 1 skein each of blue, brown, red, and white embroidery floss

Cutting

All measurements include ¼"-wide seam allowances. Appliqué patterns are on pages 109–111 and do not include seam allowances. They need to be enlarged 200%.

From the assorted tan fabrics, cut:
  • 6 squares, 13" x 13"
  • 22 squares, 1½" x 1½"
  • 1 square, 2⅞" x 2⅞"; cut in half once diagonally (only 1 triangle needed)

From the assorted blue fabrics, cut:
  • 14 small stars
  • 4 large stars
  • 1 large bat
  • 1 flag canton (star field)
  • 6" x 12" rectangle for pennant
  • 1 eagle

From the brown fabric, cut:
  • 1 dial pointer
  • Bias strips: 1" x 14" (cut on the diagonal of the 10" square) and ½" x 7"
  • 1 glove
  • 1 small bat

From the tan or off-white fabric, cut:
- 1 large baseball
- 1 small baseball
- 2 pieces, 4" x 6", for flag backgrounds
- 1 letter "B"
- 18 top bunting pieces

From the assorted gold fabrics, cut:
- 1 flagpole
- 1 flagpole top
- 10" x 12" piece for radio screen
- 1 radio knob
- "Game Today" letters
- 2 eagle talons
- 1 of each eagle banner piece

From the assorted red fabrics, cut:
- 18 bottom bunting pieces
- 14 flag stripes
- 10" x 12" piece for radio
- 2 radio bases
- 1 radio knob
- 1 pennant pole
- 1 pennant pole top
- 1 baseball cap
- 1 cap brim
- 1 cap button

From the khaki striped fabric, cut on the lengthwise grain:
- 2 border strips, 6½" x 44½"
- 2 border strips, 6½" x 42½"
- 6 sashing strips, 2½" x 12½"

From the remaining khaki fabric, cut on the crosswise grain:
- 11 sashing strips, 2½" x 12½"
- 22 squares, 1½" x 1½"
- 1 square, 2⅞" x 2⅞"; cut in half once diagonally (only 1 triangle needed)

From the remaining khaki fabric, cut on the bias:
- 2¼"-wide bias strips to yield 210" of binding

Eagle Block

1. Appliqué the shapes onto a 13" tan square in the following order: eagle (leaving the bottom of the legs free), bat, ball, talons, front banner, back banner.
2. Embroider the red stitches on the baseball using a feather stitch. Embroider the banner words and pole using an outline stitch.

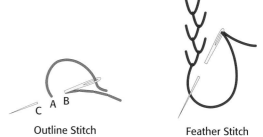

Outline Stitch   Feather Stitch

Baseball Cap Block

Appliqué the shapes onto a 13" tan square in the following order: brim, button, cap, the letter B.

Radio Block

This block uses reverse appliqué with areas cut out from the red radio fabric to allow the gold screens to show through. This technique is actually much easier than appliquéing all the gold pieces individually.

1. Transfer all the radio outlines onto freezer paper and cut out inner shapes that will become the gold areas of screen.

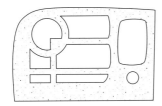

2. Iron the freezer-paper pattern onto the right side of a 10" x 12" piece of red fabric. Trace all around the radio shape, including cutouts. A white chalk pencil works well for this task.

3. Remove the paper pattern and lay the red fabric on top of a gold piece of fabric the same size. Both fabrics should be right side up. Baste the fabrics together, sewing all around the radio and around the marked shapes, taking care to leave enough space for turning under the edges of each marked shape.

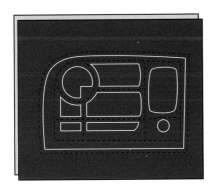

4. Starting at the dial area, carefully cut away the red fabric, taking care not to cut the gold fabric. Cut about ⅛" from the inside of the marked lines. Clip the corners and reverse appliqué along the marked line using red thread. Do not cut out the other areas until this one has been appliquéd.

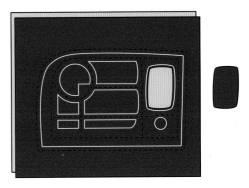

Cut out shape leaving ⅛" seam allowance. Clip corners.

5. Repeat the reverse appliqué process for each screen section, working on one area at a time. When all portions of the screen have been appliquéd, turn the red fabric over and carefully trim the gold fabric ¼" from all the stitching. Take out the basting stitches. This will leave you with a red radio with the gold fabric sewn into the screen areas. Press.

6. Trim ⅛" from the marked outside line of the radio. Position it on a 13" tan square and appliqué in place, leaving the bottom of the radio free.

7. Appliqué the red base pieces onto the bottom of the radio, covering the raw edge.

8. Appliqué the brown dial pointer, and then appliqué the red knob on top of it. Stitch the gold knob into place.

9. Embroider "…and it's Loooong Gone!" across the upper portion of the block background, using the outline stitch and brown floss.

Pennant Block

1. Appliqué the "Game Today" letters onto the 6" x 12" blue rectangle. Press. Cut out

the pennant shape from the blue fabric and appliqué it onto a 13" tan square.

2. Appliqué the pennant pole and the pole top.

3. Embroider the pennant ties using the outline stitch and blue floss.

Bat, Ball, and Glove Block

1. Appliqué the bat diagonally across a 13" tan square first. Then stitch the ball in place. Embroider red stitches onto the baseball using two strands of red floss and the feather stitch.

2. Using a ½" bias tape maker and the 1"-wide brown bias strip, make ½"-wide bias and press the completed strip. Cut this bias into four equal pieces and lay out as shown, weaving the strips together. Pin the woven bias strips in position on the background fabric.

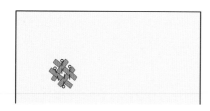

3. Using the ½"-wide brown bias strip and a ¼" bias maker, make a ¼"-wide bias strip. Pin this bias in place to create the edge of the mitt; the bias should cover the raw edges of woven webbing. Trim the ends of the webbing if needed so that they don't stick out below the ¼" bias strip. Appliqué this strip in place.

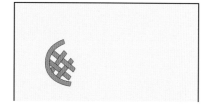

4. Position the glove so that it covers the bottom and right side of the webbing. Appliqué in place. Embroider the lines on the glove using brown floss and the outline stitch.

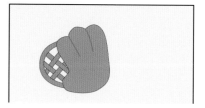

Flag Block

1. Trace the outline of the right half of the flag onto one 4" x 6" off-white piece. Do not cut it out.

2. Arrange the red stripes on the right half of the flag and appliqué the top and bottom edges of each stripe. Leave the right and left ends unsewn. Do the same for the left side of the flag.

3. Cut out the flag halves from the off-white fabric, leaving ⅛" seam allowances.

4. Appliqué the right side of the flag onto a 13" tan square. Stitch the top, right, and bottom edges, but leave the left side free.

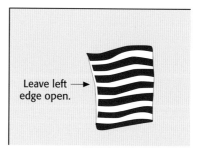

Leave left → edge open.

5. Position the left side of the flag on the tan background. The right edge of this piece should cover the raw edge of the

previously sewn flag. Appliqué in place, again leaving the left edge unsewn.

6. Appliqué the canton (blue star field) over the left piece of the flag, covering the raw edge of the stripes. Leave the left edge of the canton unsewn.

Leave left edge open.

7. Appliqué the flagpole over the raw left edge of the flag. Leave the top of the pole unsewn. Position the pole top over the pole and appliqué.

8. Embroider stars onto the canton using white floss and the star stitch (see page 123). I embroidered five rows of four stars each. Embroider "America's Pastime" onto the block background using blue floss and the outline stitch. Press.

Assembling the Quilt Top

1. Trim each block to 12½" x 12½" square.
2. Sew the 2⅞" tan and khaki triangles together to make a square. Press the seam allowances toward the darker fabric.
3. Sew each 1½" tan square to a 1½" khaki square. Press the seam allowances toward the darker fabric. Sew these units together in pairs to make 11 four-patch units. Press.
4. Lay out the appliqué blocks, sashing strips, and sashing squares (the four

patches and the one triangle square) as shown. Sew the pieces together into rows and then sew the rows together. Press.

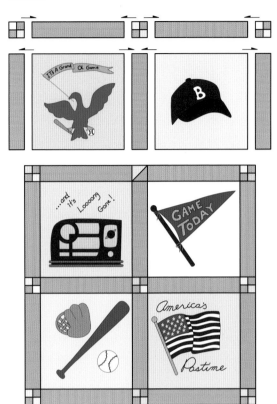

Appliquéing the Border

1. Appliqué a red bottom bunting onto a tan top bunting. Repeat 17 more times. Press.

Make 18.

2. On a 6½" x 44½" khaki strip, arrange five buntings by eye. Make sure to leave enough space all around for seam allowances on the borders, because you won't want the bunting points to be sewn into the border seam. Appliqué the buntings

in place. Then place a small star at each intersection of the buntings and appliqué. Press. Repeat for the other 6½" x 44½" strip.

3. Sew these border units to the sides of the quilt top. Press the seam allowances toward the borders.

4. Arrange four buntings on one of the 6½" x 42½" khaki strips and appliqué in place. Place a small star at each intersection of these buntings and appliqué in place. Press.

5. Sew these border units to the top and bottom of the quilt. Press the seam allowances toward the borders.

6. Place a large star at each corner intersection of the buntings and appliqué in place. Press.

Finishing the Quilt

1. Choose a quilting design and then follow the directions for marking the quilt top as described in "Quiltmaking Basics" on page 123.

2. From the backing fabric, cut two pieces, 49" long, and trim them to 32" wide. Sew them together into a 49" x 62" backing piece with a horizontal seam. Press the seam open.

3. Center and layer the quilt top and batting over the backing; baste the layers together, and then quilt as desired. The quilt shown was hand quilted with crosshatching in the background of the blocks and with leafy vines in the sashing. The borders were echo quilted to emphasize the bunting design.

4. Trim the batting and backing even with the edges of the quilt top. Use the 2¼" khaki bias strips to bind the quilt.

5. Make a label and attach it to the back of your quilt.

A native of Ann Arbor, Michigan, Laurie is an avid Detroit Tigers fan.

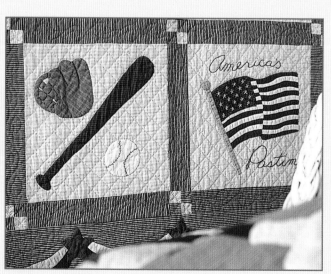

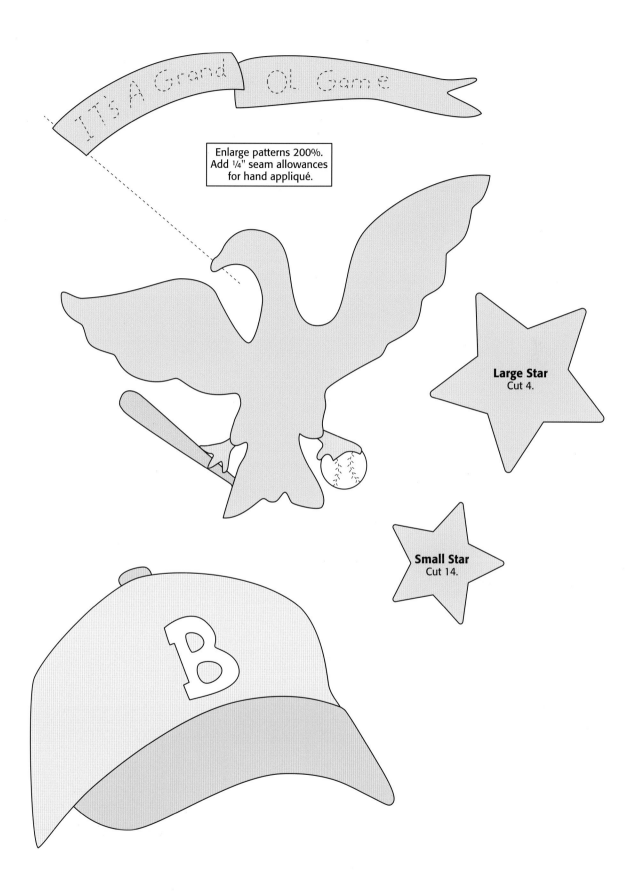

IT'S A Grand OL' Game

Enlarge patterns 200%.
Add ¼" seam allowances
for hand appliqué.

Large Star
Cut 4.

Small Star
Cut 14.

GAME TODAY

Enlarge patterns 200%.
Add ¼" seam allowances
for hand appliqué.

...and it's Loooong Gone!

Bunting Bottom Cut 18.

Bunting Top Cut 18.

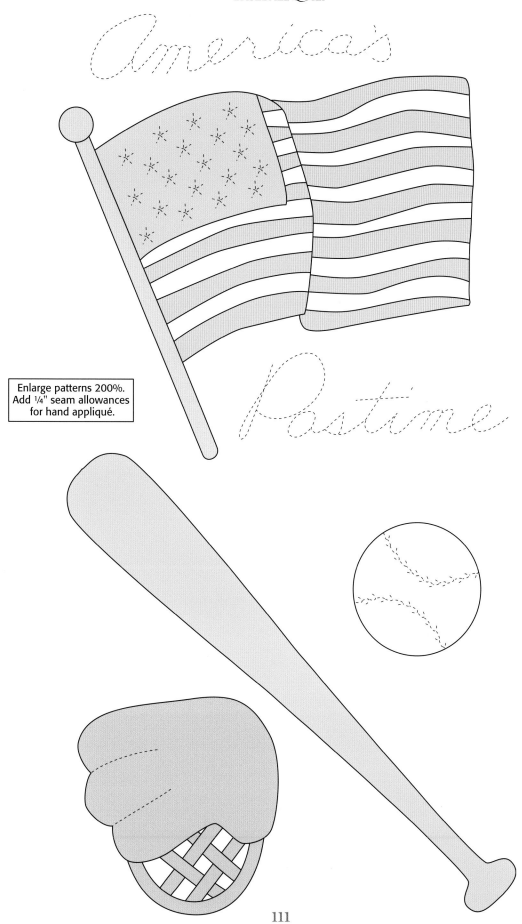

Enlarge patterns 200%.
Add ¼" seam allowances
for hand appliqué.

Finished Rug Size: 34¼" x 24¼"

Baseball Rug

Materials

Wool yardages are estimated based on 60"-wide fabric. (See "How Much Wool Do You Need?" on page 133 for more information on estimating yardage before beginning any project.)

• 1 yard total of light blue wools for backgrounds

• ¾ yard total of darker blue wools for baseball cap, pennant, flag, and eagle

• ¾ yard of medium olive green wool for border and block outlines

• ½ yard of lighter olive green wool for backgrounds

• ⅜ yard of mustard wool for background, eagle beak, and talons

• ¼ yard of light tan wool for baseball glove, bat, pennant, and flagpoles

• ¼ yard of red wool for flags and words

• ¼ yard total of assorted off-white wools for baseballs and flags

• ¼ yard of brown wool for baseball bats and glove

• 33" x 44" piece of backing fabric*

• 140" of binding tape *or* ¼ yard of fabric (as used on this rug) for binding

*If you use a hoop, add 8" to the background measurements. See "Rug Backing" on page 132 for more information on fabric-measuring techniques and backing options.

Cutting

Cut your wool into size #8 or #9 strips, referring to "Cutting the Strips" on page 133. I recommend not cutting all the wool at once; it is prone to tangle into worms. However, be sure to cut some strips of each shade to give your rug nice texture. For instance, if you have more than one light olive green wool, cut some strips of each and use a mix of them in the block backgrounds.

Making the Rug

1. Transfer the design onto your backing fabric, using the pattern (which needs to be enlarged 400%) on page 115. For details on transferring patterns, see page 132 in "Rug-Hooking Basics." Then either serge or zigzag around the edges by machine or encase the edges in masking tape to prevent raveling as you hook the rug.

2. Hook the images in the center of each block first, referring to the photograph for color placement. Note: You may want to use narrower strips for small areas, such as the webbing on the baseball glove and the red stitching on the small baseball.

3. Using medium olive green, hook a single line of loops to make the dividing lines between the blocks. Using the same wool, hook one row for the inner border to separate the blocks from the main border.

4. Hook the block backgrounds. Make sure you start by outlining each of the images with one or two strips of wool, which will give a nice random look to the backgrounds. I used mustard for the baseball cap background and light olive green for the large baseball and the bat, mitt, and ball blocks. The other three blocks have light blue backgrounds.

5. Hook a three-row border on all sides of the rug using medium olive green.

Finishing the Rug

1. Finish your rug using binding tape or with vintage ticking as I did on the rug shown. (For tips on tape application and other finishing options, see "Finishing Your Rug" on page 138.)

2. Steam and block your rug, referring to "Blocking" on page 139.

3. Sew on an identification tag, referring to "Signing Your Rug" on page 140 for various options.

Checked Stars?

If you look closely at the small flag carried by the eagle in the lower-right corner of the rug, you'll notice that I did not hook individual stars on the flag. Instead, I used a strip or two of blue-and-white checked fabric to hook the flag canton. This tricks the eye into seeing white stars on a dark blue background, and it's so much easier than trying to hook tiny little stars in a small area.

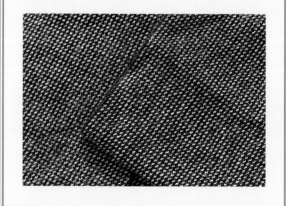

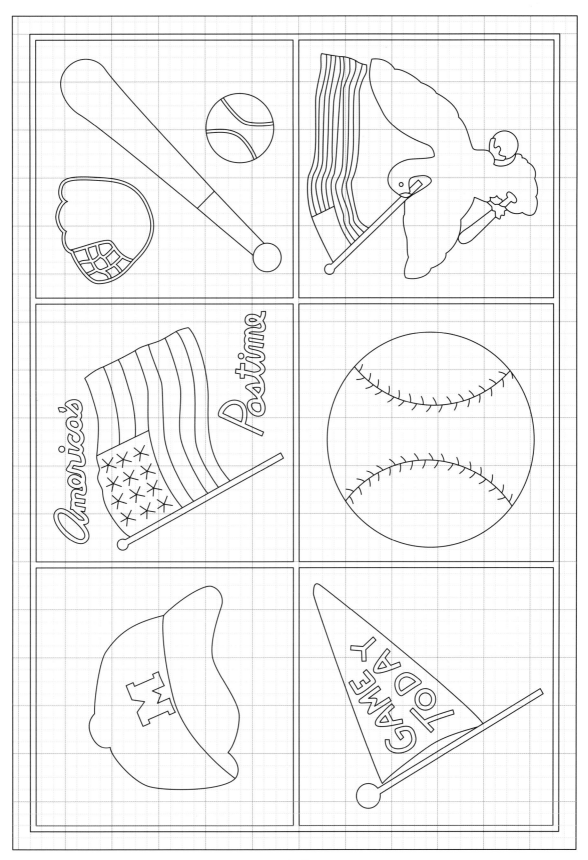

Baseball Rug
34¼" x 24¼"
1 square = ½"
Enlarge pattern 400%.

Quiltmaking Basics

I enjoy handwork, and therefore all the quilts, as well as the penny rug, in this book were done by hand. It is a relaxing and, yes, efficient way to finish your projects. Since my productivity is not limited to how much time I spend sitting in front of a sewing machine, I can get quite a lot done in a day. I hate to think of all the time I would waste at airports and hockey practices if I didn't have piecing or appliqué to keep my hands busy. However, there is no substitute for the sewing machine when certain tasks need to be accomplished. The string-pieced diamonds in "LeMoyne Star String Quilt" (page 11) were pieced by machine, as were the pieced blocks in "Log Cabin Quilt" (page 47).

But hand sewing is what drew me to quiltmaking more than 30 years ago, and I am still a fan. I hope you try at least part of the quiltmaking process by hand. I believe you will be glad you did. While I continue to be an advocate of hand piecing, hand appliqué, and hand quilting, feel free to use your favorite methods.

Laurie Simpson

Fabric

With all the time and effort we put into quilts, we should never question using the best materials we can find. Our time is worth it! The fabrics sold by quilt shops—both the brick-and-mortar merchants and the online sites—are far superior in quality to the fabrics sold by discount or chain stores. I always prefer to purchase my fabric from retailers who cater to our quilting needs. I also like to use vintage fabric when I can find it. Vintage or antique fabric scraps, if in an unused condition, can make a great addition to folk-art quilts. Vintage fabric that has been salvaged from old quilts or clothing is highly suspect. Although beautiful, it may wear much more quickly than new or unused fabric. I have taken this risk before and I was sorry I did.

Some vintage fabrics are not as colorfast as modern ones, so take care when laundering them. I prefer to wash fabric in the machine, on the gentle cycle, with very little agitation. You could also use the soak cycle. I use cool water and Orvus Paste soap, and then I dry the fabric in the dryer on the gentle/cool setting.

To prevent any unpleasant surprises, I recommend prewashing and preshrinking all fabrics—old and new. Remember to press fabric before cutting to ensure accurate measurements. All quilts in this book (except the wool quilts) are based on fabric that is 42" wide after washing.

When selecting fabric for a quilt, I like to use many fabrics rather than a single fabric to represent a particular color. For instance, in "Game Board Quilt" (page 23), I used as many as 16 different khakis for the light khaki areas. I chose as many fabrics within a close color range as possible. I believe this approach adds great depth to a quilt. There are as many as 40 different indigo fabrics in my blue and white "Snow Day Quilt" (page 75). This use of many shades of indigo allowed me to make a detailed appliqué quilt, even though it is essentially a two-color project. You can get great results with this technique.

Supplies

In addition to your sewing machine and rotary-cutting tools, here are some supplies I highly recommend.

Thread: For machine or hand piecing, use an all-purpose cotton or cotton-covered polyester thread. For appliqué, a silk-finish cotton is the most versatile. I have found that a fine (60-weight) 100%-cotton thread made for machine embroidery works great for hand appliqué. Silk appliqué thread has the benefit of being nearly invisible once sewn, but I find it difficult to work with because it is so slippery. A long-staple 100%-cotton thread is preferred for machine or hand quilting. I have recently found a 100%-silk thread that is heavy enough for hand quilting and it sews like a dream. It never tangles or knots. See "Resources" (page 142) for more information.

Needles: For hand piecing, I like size 11 Sharps. The thinner the needle, the more stitches you can put on it at once. You can use the same needle for hand appliqué, but use Betweens, which are much shorter, for hand quilting.

Pins and appliqué glue: Long, fine straight pins are a necessity for piecing. Use small sequin pins or appliqué glue with a fine-tip applicator for appliqué purposes.

Sandpaper board: This is a necessary tool for marking cloth prior to hand piecing and appliqué. Glue fine-grade sandpaper onto a hard surface such as wood or Masonite. The sandpaper holds the fabric in place while you mark it.

Scissors: Use sharp, good-quality scissors for cutting fabric. An older pair can be used to cut freezer paper or plastic templates. Small scissors with sharp tips are best for appliqué. Appliqué scissors (scissors with a wide flange) are helpful for cutting away layers of fabric from under appliqué pieces.

Template plastic: Use clear or frosted plastic (available at quilt shops) to make accurate, long-lasting templates.

Marking tools: I have a large collection of marking tools, since different fabrics require different markers. The most useful are a sharp No. 2 graphite or mechanical pencil, silver or yellow marking pencils, and chalk pencils in several colors. Be sure to keep all marking tools sharp so that your appliqué or hand-piecing seam lines are fine and accurate. Masking tape in many widths is very useful for marking straight lines on your quilt top. It's a good idea to test all marking tools on a fabric scrap before you begin your project to make certain that the marks can be removed easily.

Batting: One of the questions I'm asked most often is, "What type of batting do you use?" The desired look of the quilt and the ease of quilting are the most important factors to consider when choosing quilt batting. Machine quilters generally favor a flat cotton batting. For hand quilting, polyester batting is easier to needle, but most quilters prefer cotton or a cotton blend for the look and drape of the quilt. For my quilts, I prefer Hobbs 100% Organic Cotton Batting because it most closely replicates the look of an antique quilt after it has been washed.

To replicate the look of a traditional

antique quilt, use 100%-cotton batting without scrim. (Scrim is a layer used to hold the cotton layers together, but it can add stiffness and make hand quilting more difficult.) After the quilt is washed, this type of batting will shrink about 3%–5%. When the batting shrinks, a small pucker appears around each quilting stitch, creating the look and feel of a well-loved antique. Remember to factor in this shrinkage when planning the size of your finished quilt.

Bias tape maker: This handy notion makes quick work of bias stems and other long, narrow pieces that need to curve. The finished bias widths needed for the quilts in this book are ½" and ¼". Cut bias strips twice the width of the finished bias and feed them in one end of the bias maker. A folded, finished bias tape comes out the other end. Press the bias immediately and it is ready to be appliquéd.

Additional supplies: Other useful supplies include tracing paper, freezer paper, a needle threader, thimble, finger cots, tape measure, and seam ripper. And, of course, you will need an iron for pressing.

Rotary Cutting

Using a rotary cutter, a cutting mat, and an acrylic ruler will allow you to cut your fabric pieces more accurately and more quickly than using scissors. The following steps describe how to rotary cut a 2" square.

1. Fold the fabric with the selvages together and align the fabric horizontally on a line on the cutting mat. Using a 6" x 24" clear acrylic ruler and your rotary cutter, make a fresh cut perpendicular to the selvage to make a straight edge.

2. Move the ruler so that 2" of the fabric shows beneath it.

3. After the strip is cut, pivot the cutting mat so that the strip is horizontal to you. Cut the strip into 2" pieces to make 2" x 2" squares.

Piecing

While I prefer to piece by hand, I realize that many people like to machine piece, so I've covered the basics of each technique here.

Hand Piecing

Despite being a little out of fashion, hand piecing can be a very efficient way to make a quilt. Instead of waiting for a time when you can be in your sewing room, you can hand piece nearly anywhere. Aided by a small portable sewing kit, you can stitch quilt blocks during breaks at work, while watching TV, or when you're traveling.

1. Rotary cut fabric pieces with a ¼" seam allowance added, just as for machine piecing. Lay the cut fabric on a sandpaper board to keep the fabric from distorting and to reduce pressure on the marking tool. Use a 1" x 12" acrylic ruler and a marking pencil to mark a scant ¼" (to take the width of the marked line into account) seam allowance onto the wrong side of each piece.

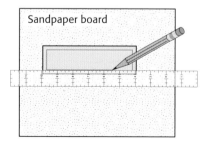

Mark stitching line.

2. The marked line is your sewing line. Use a sharp needle and cotton piecing thread to sew a small running stitch (about $\frac{1}{16}$" long) on the line. Don't knot the thread at the end; take a small backstitch on top of your first stitch to secure it. Start and stop at the sewing lines. Do not sew into the seam allowances.

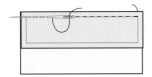

3. To end the sewing line, take a small stitch on top of your last stitch and then make a knot in the thread. Pull the knot down with your fingernail so that it is right up against the fabric, and pull to secure it. When you reach an intersection of seam lines, make an extra stitch to anchor your pieces. Check occasionally to be sure you're sewing on the line on both the front and back. Also, take a backstitch every time you fill a needle with stitches—about every 1" to 1$\frac{1}{2}$".

Machine Piecing

If you prefer to machine piece your quilt, you do not have to mark the stitching line on your patches. Each project gives cutting directions that include the $\frac{1}{4}$" seam allowance on all pieces. You simply need to maintain a consistent $\frac{1}{4}$"-wide seam allowance as you feed the patches through your machine. Otherwise the blocks will not be the desired finished size, and the sashing or border pieces will not fit properly.

Some machines have a special presser foot that measures exactly $\frac{1}{4}$" from the center of the needle position to the edge of the foot.

In this case, you can use the edge of the foot to guide your fabric. If your machine doesn't have such a foot, create a seam guide by placing the edge of a piece of tape or moleskin $\frac{1}{4}$" from the needle.

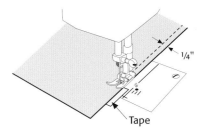

Pressing

For accurate piecing, whether by hand or machine, it's important to press seams to one side, usually toward the darker fabric. First press the seam flat to set the stitching, and then press the seam allowance in the desired direction. Press carefully. Don't push the iron back and forth, as this can distort the fabric pieces.

Hand Appliqué

Needle-turn appliqué is my preferred appliqué method. Since so little preparation is required, I think it's the most time-efficient method—and the most portable. Feel free to substitute an appliqué technique you prefer. *The Easy Art of Appliqué* by Mimi Dietrich and Roxi Eppler (That Patchwork Place, 1994) is an excellent reference that covers hand-, machine-, and fusible-appliqué methods. The following steps describe the basic technique for performing hand appliqué. Please note that templates for appliqué do not include seam allowances.

1. Draw around the appliqué template to mark your sewing line. Cut $\frac{1}{8}$" from this line. Pin or use appliqué glue to hold the piece in place.

Cutting Wool Shapes

Adding a seam allowance to appliqués is necessary for cotton fabrics only. For wool appliqué, cut the fabric exactly on the marked line. Wool doesn't need to be turned under because it doesn't fray.

2. Use a single strand of thread and an appliqué needle (also known as a Sharp) to sew the piece into place. Starting on a straight edge or gentle curve, use the tip of the needle to turn under the seam allowance on the marked line. Turn under only about ½" ahead of where your needle comes up. Turn under just enough for only the next four or five stitches. Work from right to left if you are right-handed, and hold the turned seam allowance between the thumb and forefinger of your left hand as you take small appliqué stitches. If you are left-handed, work from left to right and hold the work in your right hand. A seam allowance that will be covered by another piece does not need to be sewn down.

3. The appliqué stitch is worked from right to left (if you are right-handed). Begin by sewing up through the background fabric and into the crease of the seam allowance of the appliqué piece. Insert the needle into the background directly next to where it came into the appliqué piece. Let the needle travel about 1/16" to the left of the previous stitch, and again come up into the crease of the folded edge (or a thread or two into the appliqué piece). Keep your stitches taut, but don't pull so tightly that the fabric puckers.

4. To end the stitching, pull the needle to the wrong side of the fabric. Take two small stitches into the background fabric behind the appliqué piece. Don't let these stitches show on the front. Make a knot and clip the thread, leaving a ½" tail.

Appliquéing Outside Points

Begin taking smaller stitches closer together when you approach an outside point. When you reach the point, take a stitch directly at the point, and then use the tip of your needle to push the seam allowance under it and toward the side already sewn. Trim away some of the seam allowance, if necessary, for a perfect point. Continue to appliqué as before.

Appliquéing Inside Points

You will need to clip the seam allowance into the point so that you can turn the fabric under on each side of the point. Then, when approaching an inside point, start taking smaller, closer stitches about ¼" before the point. Stitch past the point, return, and make another stitch at that point, stitching into the appliqué piece by a few more threads to hold it securely.

Glue Basting for Appliqué

Although you can pin or thread baste your appliqué shapes in place on the background, glue basting is an effective technique for needle-turn appliqué. It allows appliqué pieces to lie very flat against the background and has the benefit of no pins to catch your thread as you stitch. Use washable, water-based fabric glue, such as *Roxanne's Glue-Baste-It*, with a very fine applicator tip. You need only a few dots of glue to secure the fabric. The glue will wash out easily after your quilt is finished.

Bias Strips for Appliqué

An easy way to make the bias strips for "Baseball Quilt" (page 103) is to use a bias maker. You can find this tool at your local quilt shop or online. The following instructions are for finished ½"-wide bias strips.

1. Use a rotary cutter, a cutting mat, and an acrylic ruler to cut a piece of fabric on the bias into 1"-wide strips.

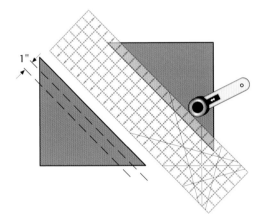

2. Pass the bias strip through the bias maker. If it does not pass easily, cut the starting end to a point and force it through using a pin or stiletto in the center groove.

3. Pull the bias maker along the strip while ironing the folded end of the strip as you go.

Reverse Appliqué

Reverse appliqué is just as easy as regular appliqué, so don't be intimidated. It's often easier to use this technique, which involves cutting away part of the top fabric to let the underneath fabric show, rather than trying to appliqué a small shape on top. Here is how to reverse appliqué the radio screen for the "Baseball Quilt."

1. After you have basted the red radio fabric on top of the gold screen fabric, cut a slit into the screen area. Cut only the top piece of fabric, not the background (screen) area. Cut away the inside area, leaving a ⅛" seam allowance.

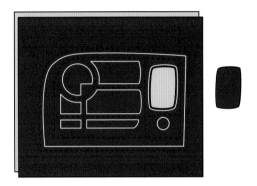

2. Snip at each corner of cutaway area up to the seam line.

3. With your needle, tuck each side of the screen sections under until the fabric is pushed under the drawn line. Appliqué on this line all the way around as you would for regular needle-turn appliqué.

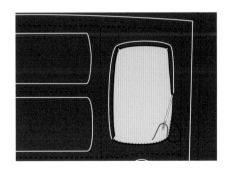

4. After all the reverse appliqué is complete, turn the appliqué block to the back and carefully cut away the underneath fabric from the areas where it is still behind the top fabric, leaving ¼" seam allowances. This will make your block lighter, more flexible, and easier to quilt through.

Prairie Points

Prairie points create a decorative edge that offers an alternative way to bind your quilt. This technique was used for both "Folky Animals Quilt" (page 35) and "Nautical Wool Quilt" (page 91).

1. Cut a square of cotton fabric as described in the quilt directions. Fold this square in half diagonally with the wrong sides together. Fold the triangle diagonally again to form a smaller triangle. Press after each fold. Repeat for all the cotton squares.

2. Tuck the fold of one prairie point into the opening of the first one. You can have them overlap as much or as little as you wish. Arrange by eye along the edge of your quilt.

3. Pin the points in place on your quilt top, with the points facing toward the center of your quilt and the raw edges aligned. Sew the prairie points to all four edges of your quilt top, stitching ¼" from the

edges. On the wool quilts in this book, a large stitch length will work best.

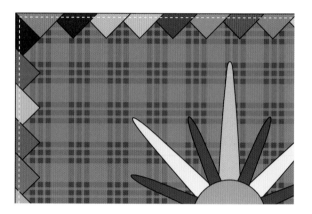

4. When quilting your project, make sure to leave ½" unquilted around the entire edge of the quilt top for turning under the seam allowances of the prairie points and quilt backing. When quilting is complete, trim the batting even with the edges of the quilt top. Trim the backing fabric so that it is ½" larger than the quilt top all around.

5. Flip the prairie points up and away from the quilt center so that the seam allowance is folded over the batting. Then fold under the ½" seam allowance on the backing and whipstitch the edges closed.

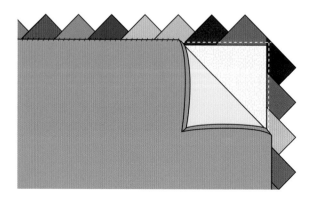

Embroidery Details

Some of the quilts in this book have embroidery details. The specific stitches are described and shown here.

Outline stitch: The outline stitch appears in several places on "Baseball Quilt" (page 103). To make the stitch, bring the needle up from behind the fabric and put the needle back down approximately ⅛" to the right. Bring the needle back through at the midpoint of the stitch you just made, coming up at the bottom side of the stitch.

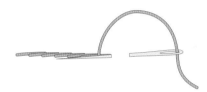

Blanket stitch: This stitch is used to secure the wool appliqué pieces in "Folky Animals Quilt" and "Nautical Wool Quilt."

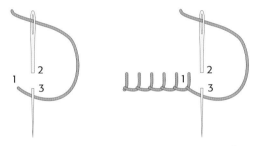

Star stitch: The star stitch is used in "Sailor Penny Rug" (page 61) and "Baseball Quilt."

Bring needle up at 1 and down at 2.

Bring needle up at 3 and down at 2.

Bring needle up at 4 and down at 2, up at 5 and down at 2, up at 6 and down at 2.

Feather stitch: This stitch is used to replicate the seams of the baseball on "Baseball Quilt."

Marking the Quilt Top

After you have decided on a quilt design, mark the design onto your quilt top with a marking tool that can be washed away after your quilt is finished. Refer to "Supplies" on page 117 for suggested marking tools, and make sure you test your tools on fabric scraps before using them.

Layering and Basting the Quilt

After the top is marked, layer the top, batting, and backing into a quilt "sandwich." The quilt backing and batting must be at least 4" larger than the quilt top. If the backing is pieced, press the seam allowances open for easier quilting.

1. Spread the backing, wrong side up, on a clean flat surface. Secure the edges with masking tape. Keep the back smooth, but do not stretch it too tightly.
2. Spread the batting over the backing, smoothing out any wrinkles. Lay the quilt top over the batting and smooth it out, keeping the quilt-top edges square with the backing and batting.

3. Baste the sandwich together with needle and thread, rustproof safety pins, or a basting spray (following manufacturer's directions). When basting with thread or pins, do so in a large grid pattern spaced every 6" to 8". I also like to baste all around the perimeter of the quilt top, approximately 1¼" from the edge, to keep the edges square and secure.

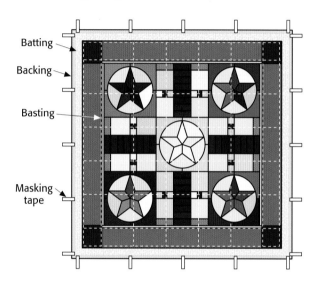

Batting

Backing

Basting

Masking tape

Hand Quilting

1. Thread a quilting needle with about 18" of hand-quilting thread, and make a small knot at the end of the thread. Insert the needle into the top layer of the quilt, about ½" from where you want to start the quilting stitches. Push the needle through the top and batting (but not the backing). Bring the needle up at the quilting line. Gently tug on the thread until the knot is buried into the quilt backing.

2. Make small, even running stitches through all the quilt layers on the marked quilting line.

3. To end your quilting thread, place the needle down near the point where the quilting thread comes out of the quilt. Wrap the thread around the needle three times. Put the needle back into the quilt top and batting (not the backing), one stitch length away. Bring the needle up approximately ½" and gently tug on the quilting thread until the knot you made is buried into the quilt batting. Clip the thread. For more instructions on hand quilting, read *Loving Stitches: A Guide to Fine Hand Quilting* by Jeanna Kimball (Martingale & Company, 2004).

Machine Quilting

All of the quilts in this book are quilted by hand. If you prefer to quilt by machine (and since I am not a machine quilter), I recommend *Machine Quilting Made Easy* by Maurine Noble (Martingale & Company, 1994) as a guide on the subject.

Binding

Once you have finished quilting your project, trim the batting and backing even with the quilt top. To make a straight-grain binding, cut enough 2¼"-wide strips to go around all sides of your quilt plus an extra 6"–8". To make bias binding, as was used for the striped binding on "Baseball Quilt" (page 103), simply cut your strips on the bias, using the 45° line on your rotary-cutting ruler as a guide. Join the strips in one continuous length, using a diagonal seam to help distribute bulk. Pressing the seam allowances open will also help distribute bulk.

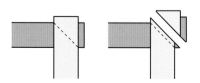

Joining Straight-Grain Strips

1. Fold the strip in half lengthwise with the wrong sides together. Press. Starting on one side of the quilt (not at a corner), sew the binding to the quilt front using a ¼" seam allowance. Stop stitching ¼" from the corner of the quilt. Backstitch and cut the thread.

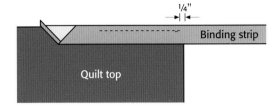

2. Turn the quilt so that you can sew along the next side. Fold the binding up away from the quilt, and then fold the binding back down upon itself. There will be a triangle of excess binding at the corner.

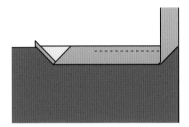

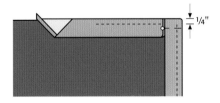

3. Begin to stitch again along the next side of the quilt, again using a ¼" seam allowance. Backstitch at the beginning to secure your stitches, but stop stitching ¼" from the top and right edges of the quilt.

4. Repeat the process for each corner. When you're within 3" to 4" of the beginning of the binding, tuck the starting edge into the end of the binding. Fold the end of the binding up ¼" so there is no raw edge. Trim if needed. Finish stitching the binding to the quilt.

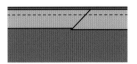

5. Fold the binding over the raw edge of the quilt and sew the folded edge onto the quilt back using an appliqué stitch. A miter will form naturally at each corner as you fold the binding into place.

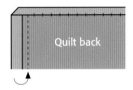
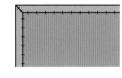

Labeling the Quilt

It's important to label your quilt so the recipient and future generations will know the story behind it. You can make a plain fabric label, or you can repeat a design from the front of the quilt, as I often like to do. Use a permanent fabric marker (or embroidery) to sign your name, date, and any other pertinent information about your quilt on the label fabric. Appliqué the label onto the back of your quilt.

Rug-Hooking Basics

Any time you work on a rug, you are making a potential heirloom, so give your rug the attention to detail it deserves. I find that working with tools I love and quality materials makes the process enjoyable and the end result a rug to be cherished.

In this section you will find a review of the tools and supplies you'll need, as well as how-to information and tips on basic rug-hooking and finishing techniques. For more information, you may want to take a look at the previous book Laurie and I collaborated on, *Folk Art Friends* (Martingale & Company, 2003).

Polly Minick

Supplies

High-quality materials are worth the investment. Most of the following can be purchased at fabric specialty stores and on the Internet. While I have my favorites, what works well for you might be different from what works best for me. So if possible, try out various hooks, frames, and hoops before you commit. Remember to always use good lighting when rug hooking. I use an Ott-Lite, which is a great help in seeing true colors.

Hook: Hook selection is very personal. The handles vary from ball style to straight handle to very slim pencil styles, so you can choose the type that fits best in your hand. The hooks also vary, from narrow to wide shanks, and from rounded to blunt to pointed tips. For the folk-art or primitive-style rugs in this book, choose a hook with a sturdy shank for hooking wool up to ¼" wide. Some of the more popular hooks on the market now have a very pointed end; personally, I find this type of hook doesn't work with my hooking style. Other hookers love them. If you ever have the opportunity to attend a rug-hooking camp or hook-in, look around—you'll see that very few people ever use the same hook. So try a hook first and work with it a bit to be sure it feels right for you.

Machine cloth cutter or rotary cutter: You can cut wool strips using the same rotary cutter, mat, and acrylic ruler you use for quilting. I find that most people who go from quiltmaking to rug hooking are more adept at using the rotary cutter for a while, until they decide just how much rug hooking they are going to do. I also find that people who have not made quilts are not quite as willing to give the rotary-cutting method a go, but it works great and is worth a try.

Once you've become a dedicated rug hooker, you may want to invest in a cloth cutter to cut your wool strips easily and accurately. Rigby, Bliss, Fraser, Bolivar, and Townsend cutters all make cutting a breeze. The Townsend cutter is the newest on the market and I love how easily the different sizes of cutting heads snap into place. It also comes with extra heads and a handy carrying case for the cutter, which makes it great for traveling to classes and rug camps too. (See "Resources" on page 142.)

Wool: The preferred fabric for making hooked rugs is 100% wool. You can find wool yardage at fabric stores, quilt shops, and at online sites. You can also use vintage wool from used garments, so check around at yard sales and thrift stores too.

Rug backing: You can use burlap, monk's cloth, or linen as backing fabric for hooked rugs. For more on each of these choices, see "Rug Backing" on page 132.

Hoop or frame: You will need to hold the backing fabric taut as you hook. You can do that by loading it either in a traditional quilting hoop or onto a rug-hooking frame. Frames come in both lap and floor models. Most have gripper teeth to hold the fabric taut and make loading and unloading easy. I started out with a hoop and continue to use the same hoop today. I'm certainly in a minority as far as using a hoop is concerned. People are often surprised that I have made all my rugs in this hoop, but I make even large, room-size rugs in that same hoop. It is what works wonderfully for me.

Rug binding: Just as with quilts, hooked rugs need to have their edges finished. Finishing will prevent the backing fabric from fraying and give a nice, neat edge to your rug. You can bind the edges of your rug in a variety of ways, including using rug-binding tape or strips of fabric, and whipping around the edges with wool strips or yarn. For more on these options and how to attach them to your rug, see "Finishing Your Rug" on page 138.

Scissors: You'll need basic fabric scissors for snipping off the ends of wool strips and for cutting your backing fabric.

Black permanent marker: You will need one of these for transferring printed patterns or your own designs onto your rug backing.

Red-Dot tracer medium: This tracing material is available at most fabric stores. It is used to trace full-size paper patterns or to draw original patterns and then transfer them onto backing fabric. The dotted grid will help you align your patterns with the grain of your backing fabric.

Graph paper: You will find this handy for sketching designs. It makes enlarging initial sketches easier because you can use the grid as a sizing guideline. You can also use graph paper to enlarge the patterns in this book if you prefer to do that manually rather than using a photocopier.

Optional Supplies

If (or should I say when!) you want to try your hand at dying wool, you'll need the following supplies.

Dyes and dye formulas: Cushing and Pro-Chem make the most reliable dyes for wool. You'll also need a formula book (available at local quilt shops, rug-hooking stores, bookstores, or online retailers) that will specify exactly how much of each pigment to add to the mix to get the colors you want.

Dye equipment: You'll need a large pot, rubber gloves, wooden spoons, tongs, and vinegar for setting the color. Some people are now using citric acid instead of vinegar, as they find it easier to keep on hand than large jugs of vinegar. Of course, equipment used for dyeing wool will be used exclusively for this purpose.

Color wheel: This handy device will help in planning your wool colors. Look for one at your local paint or art-supply store.

Rug-hooking periodicals: You may also want to check out *Rug Hooking* and *Wool Street Journal* for help in finding supplies, books, teachers, rug camps, and other important information related to this art.

All About Wool

When I lecture on rug hooking, participants are always full of questions about wool, from where to find it and what type of wool to use, to how to measure, cut, and store it. Since the foundation of rug hooking is fabric, and wool is the preferred choice, it's well worth spending time to learn more about this wonderful fiber.

Where to Find Wool

Perhaps you're lucky enough to live near a quilt or fabric shop that carries wool for rug hooking. You can also buy new wool direct from woolen mills and via the Internet. In addition to using new wool, you can recycle wool. I'm particularly fond of vintage wool. Finding it is not always easy, so getting your hands on the perfect piece is quite a luxury. Some of the best places to find wool clothing are thrift shops, flea markets, garage sales—and even in your own attic. Using Grandpa's old plaid wool shirt or a great-aunt's skirt in a rug is a nice way to remember him or her. But be careful about "shopping" at home. Your family members may not be quite so happy to see their current favorite shirts transformed into a rug!

Be selective about buying wool clothing. Sometimes no matter how little you have to pay, it still is not a bargain. For instance, I don't recommend gabardine wool, which is often found in suits. It's flat, slick, and it ravels. Suit jackets and sport coats also usually have interfacing glued to the inside for shaping which makes them unusable. Any loosely woven wool will make hooking difficult. So what should you look for?

- Skirts are usually the best choice, as they yield more fabric with fewer seams to undo.
- The backs of wool shirts also provide a nice-size chunk of wool you can use for hooking, and they're a good way to find plaids.
- Check the label to make sure the garment is 100% wool. At the very least, 80% wool and 20% other fiber content is acceptable. Anything less than the traditional 80–20 blend will cause you more grief than it is worth.

Preparing Your Wool

Whether vintage or new, it's important to make sure your wool is clean and dry before using or storing it. This is particularly important when using vintage wool pieces you have picked up at rummage sales and flea markets. Make sure you wash it immediately before you do anything else. I like to first wash the garments and then take them apart and wash the pieces again before storing them. Remember, moths only eat wool when it's dirty. Protect your wool stash, your rugs, and your wool wardrobe by always washing your wool finds as soon as you bring them home.

Wash wool by machine using a mild detergent and regular cold-water wash settings. I usually dry the wool completely in the dryer, but you can also dry it for just a few minutes, so it is fluffy but still damp, and then hang it up to finish drying. You will be amazed at what a wonderful treatment washing and drying is for your wool. (And you'll be equally amazed by the amount of lint it creates, so be sure to clean out the lint trap after each load.)

At least some time in the dryer is important for removing the wrinkles from the washing process. The damp-dry method is a good way to ensure that you will not felt your wool, thereby making it too thick to use for hooking. I've found that the dryer very seldom felts my wool, but there is no guarantee. After the wool is dry, it's ready to be used as is, stored for future use, or overdyed.

Storing Wool

If possible, store your wool in a room or closet set aside strictly for that purpose. Being able to see the wool and all the glorious colors is not only a joy but also helpful when planning the colors for your next project. So even if you need to keep your wool in a closet, it's a good idea to stow it in clear plastic bins or on open shelves so that you can see exactly what you have. I have tried all ways of storing wool over the years, and I currently have mine displayed in an antique wine bin. Not only is the bin a delight to see when I am working in my studio, but I can tell at a glance what I have and which colors are getting low. It makes designing projects, hooking rugs, and keeping track of inventory so much easier.

Dyeing to Get the Right Colors

While the scope of this book can't begin to cover the intricacies of dyeing wool, I do want to mention a little bit about overdyeing wool. You can certainly use "as-is" wool (wash it, cut it, and hook with it, just the way it is). Some artists use almost all as-is wool and their work is beautiful. Personally, I prefer duller colors than what I can usually find on the bolt, and because I feel the more muted colors work best in my style of rugs, I have always felt the need to tone down colors a bit before I use them. Overdyeing wool is the best way for me to achieve the colors I like.

To merely tone down a color, place the wool in a dye formula for the color exactly opposite the original wool color on the color wheel. For example, if you find bright red wool that's of great quality and an even better price, but the color is too bright for your rug, you can tone down the color by placing it in a bath of green dye formula. Why? Because green is the color opposite red on the color wheel. Start with a very weak solution to tone down the color just a bit, and add some more formula if needed to achieve the color that pleases you.

Color Wheel Hang Up

I like to always hang my color wheel in the same position (with the same color at the top) so at a quick glance I can find the opposite color with no confusion. In no time, you'll be an old hand at color opposites.

A more radical way to overdye wool is by completely changing the color. Light-colored wools such as off-white, cream, oatmeal, light gray, and tan can be transformed quite easily into darker colors. Flannel skirts in tan or gray are readily available, but it's not nearly as easy to find them in old gold or a nice medium blue. Checks, plaids, tweeds, and other patterns that have a light-colored background always lend themselves nicely to overdyeing. The light area will take on the new color, but the dark part of the fabric will remain.

If you'd like to dye wool, your best bet is to use Pro Chem MX Reactive Dyes and Cushing Perfection Acid Dyes, which are available at some quilt shops as well as online. Both of these dyes are acid dyes for natural fibers. (See "Resources" on page 142 for ordering information.) Pro Chem dyes are sold in jars of primary colors and you mix the colors to get the exact tone of a color you want. Cushing dyes are sold in little packets of premixed pigments and are available in a wide range of colors and shades.

There are several good books on dyeing wool available at your local bookstore, quilt shop, or online. If you're interested in dyeing wool, I'd recommend reading one of these books for how-to information. Not only do they cover all the equipment you'll need (such as special measuring spoons for dye) and basic dyeing techniques but they also provide a wide range of specific color recipes. A particular book you may enjoy is *Purely Primitive* by Pat Cross (Martingale & Company, 2003). Pat's book has patterns for primitive rugs as well as a section on dyeing wool.

If you'd like to re-create some of my favorite colors to use in your rugs, you'll find the recipes on the facing page.

Learning to Dye

If you haven't tried dyeing your own wool yet, and you're hesitant to try or not sure if you'll enjoy the process, you might want to take a class at a rug camp. I hooked many rugs before I started dyeing wool. I was very intimidated by the thought of dyeing, even though I knew it would help me get the exact colors I wanted. Probably the most important milestone of my rug-hooking career was when I was invited to accompany two friends to Vermont, where we were fortunate enough to learn from noted rug hooker and dyeing guru Maryanne Lincoln. Hands-on learning with a patient and talented teacher was a terrific experience, and one I'll always value. If you, too, are a little afraid of jumping into wool dyeing or you aren't sure where to start, consider taking a dyeing class and learning how to create any color wool you wish!

Polly's Dye-Book Formulas

All of the formulas below use Pro Chem dyes except for
"Polly's Favorite Red" which uses Cushing dyes.

POLLY'S FAVORITE RED
1 full packet of Terra Cotta
½ teaspoon American Beauty
½ teaspoon Mahogany
¼ teaspoon Buttercup Yellow

DORSET RED
9/64 teaspoon #338 Red
3/128 teaspoon #489 Blue
3/128 teaspoon #119 Yellow

OLD RED
*Thanks to Maryanne Lincoln for
this recipe.*

¾ teaspoon #233 Orange
½ + 1/64 teaspoon #338 Red
¼ + 1/128 teaspoon #119 Yellow
⅛ teaspoon #672 Black
1/32 teaspoon #487 Blue

MY BEST ALL-TIME BLUE
This is the only blue you may
ever need! Just vary the amounts
of blue and black for light,
medium, and dark blue. Use
over grays and off-whites for
several shades of blue. Over
camel and tan wools, you'll
achieve various shades of bluish
green.

Lightest blue:
¼ teaspoon each of #672
Black and #490 Blue
Light to medium blue:
½ teaspoon each of #672
Black and #490 Blue
Medium to dark blue:
¾ teaspoon each of #672
Black and #490 Blue

Darkest blue:
1 teaspoon each of #672 Black
and #490 Blue

VERMONT BLUE
⅛ + ¼ teaspoon #490 Blue
⅛ teaspoon #672 Black
1/32 teaspoon #338 Red
1/64 teaspoon #119 Yellow

STONEWARE COBALT BLUE
¼ + ⅛ teaspoon #490 Blue
⅛ teaspoon #672 Black
1/32 teaspoon #338 Red
1/64 teaspoon #119 Yellow

For darker Cobalt Blue, change
amounts to:
½ teaspoon #490 Blue
¼ teaspoon #672 Black

SOFT BLUE GREEN*
3/16 teaspoon #672 Black
⅛ teaspoon #487 Blue
*This is a blue dye that creates
bluish green when used over
camel or tan wools.*

POLLY'S KHAKI
⅛ teaspoon #672 Black
⅛ teaspoon #119 Yellow

**MARINE CORPS
BLANKET KHAKI**
1½ teaspoons #135 Yellow
½ teaspoon #119 Yellow
½ teaspoon #672 Black
¼ teaspoon #728N Green
⅛ teaspoon #338 Red

**VERMONT HONEY
MUSTARD***
⅜ teaspoon #119 Yellow
¼ teaspoon #233 Orange
3/16 teaspoon #672 Black
1/64 + 1/128 teaspoon #487
Blue
1/64 teaspoon #338 Red
1/128 teaspoon #490 Blue
*This is the best mustard, but
the chemicals in the water
in some regions can make it
greenish or brassy.*

NEW KHAKI
¼ teaspoon #119 Yellow
⅛ teaspoon #672 Black
⅛ teaspoon #233 Orange
1/32 teaspoon #487 Blue

KHAKI GREEN
⅜ teaspoon #672 Black
⅜ teaspoon #119 Yellow
3/16 teaspoon #728 Green

Rug Backing

You have essentially three choices when it comes to rug-backing fabric: Scottish burlap, monk's cloth, and primitive linen. I've listed them in order from least to most expensive. All of them are suitable for rug backing, but like everything else, you may have a strong personal preference for one type over the other.

Most early rugs were hooked on burlap. Rug hookers were frugal and used what was readily available—feed sacks. That is why so many early rugs are somewhat the same size. I started out using burlap, as many artists did, as that was what was available in the late 1970s. Today I hook on linen because I hook every day and the feel of this fabric is so much softer than burlap on my hands. If the burlap works fine for you, go ahead and use it.

Monk's cloth is a mid-priced option, and it's also softer than burlap. Many of my friends use it, so I felt the need to try it. I quickly realized that it was not for me, because it did not stay taut in my hoop and that slowed down my hooking. However, if you use a frame with a gripper system, you might love working with monk's cloth.

When preparing your backing fabric, make sure it is at least 8" larger than your finished rug dimensions so that you can load it onto a rug-hooking frame. If you are using a hoop for hooking, your fabric should be at least 16" larger. It is a good idea to either tape around the edges with masking tape or serge or zigzag the edges on a sewing machine to prevent the edges from raveling when working on your rug.

Getting Ready to Hook

Before you can hook loops of wool through the backing fabric, you'll need to transfer the pattern onto the backing fabric, select the wool for the project, and cut the wool into strips.

Transferring Patterns

All of the rug patterns in this book need to be enlarged. We've presented the patterns as complete rug designs, drawn to scale but greatly reduced in size. You can use the grid behind the pattern as a guide for enlarging the pattern by hand, or you can take the pattern to your local copy shop and ask them to enlarge it by the percentage indicated on the pattern. Either way, you need to make a full-size pattern.

1. Place the full-sized paper pattern on a flat surface and lay a sheet of Red-Dot transfer paper over the design. Tape the transfer paper in place and trace the design with a black permanent marker, being careful to trace over the entire design.

2. Lay the sheet of Red-Dot paper on top of the backing fabric, making sure the pattern is squared up with the grain lines of the fabric. This will make it easier to hook straight lines of color in your pattern, while ensuring that your finished rug will lie flat and square. Tape the pattern in place and trace over it again with the black marker. For this step, go over the design using a somewhat heavy hand so that the ink seeps through the transfer paper onto your backing fabric.

3. When you lift the Red-Dot paper from the backing fabric, the design on the backing fabric may be quite faint. Trace over the design again with the marker so that the outline is very clear. Make sure that all of the design lines have been transferred.

How Much Wool Do You Need?

The yardage requirements for the projects in this book are all based on four times the area to be covered. Depending on how closely together you pack your loops and how high you pull your loops, you may find you will need closer to five times the area. The yardages are based on the amount of wool I needed to complete the rugs.

Cutting the Strips

Most rug hookers use a cloth or strip cutter to cut their wool, but you can also use a rotary cutter and ruler if you do not have a strip cutter.

The strip width is referred to by a numbering system used for the strip cutters, rather than by dimensions. So even if you don't use a strip cutter, you will need to know how the system works. There are four or five major brands of cutters. Most of the models cut fabric into two or three strips at a time. They all use the same numbering system, although the actual strip width may vary a little bit from one brand to another. Basically the number associated with the strip width represents increments in 32nds of an inch, as

When You Run Out of Wool

If you're new to rug hooking, you may be a little nervous about running out of a color because you don't have a lot of experience in measuring and judging the amounts needed. This does happen, and in my experience, it's most often in the background color where you run short. Here's a trick you can try to make your background fabric go further: add more motifs to the rug design!

Many years ago I hooked a primitive pot of flowers that was turning out nicely—until I ran out of the background color. Since this was before I started dyeing wool, there was no way for me to make more of the color I needed. I simply added a couple of primitive flowers to fill in some of the background space, rather than pulling out all the background loops and starting over with a new—and bigger—piece of wool.

That solution may not work for every rug design, so another option is to "make do" by adding another color into your background mix. If you look closely at very early rugs you'll see that their makers often used different colors in a background, and the colors weren't necessarily used randomly for a blended look. Rug backgrounds had actual blotches of different colors. I like that old look, so now if I were to run out, I would make do and add another color.

shown in the following chart.

Strip Size	Strip Width
#3	$^3/_{32}$"
#4	$^4/_{32}$" ($^1/_8$")
#5	$^5/_{32}$"
#6	$^6/_{32}$" ($^3/_{16}$")
#7	$^7/_{32}$"
#8	$^8/_{32}$" ($^1/_4$")
#9	$^9/_{32}$"
#10	$^{10}/_{32}$" ($^5/_{16}$")

Most primitive-style rug hookers cut their strips to sizes #6 through #10, while traditional rug hookers use sizes #3 through #6. Almost all machines on the market have cutter blades available in a range from a #2 to a #9 or #10 cut. I always use a #8 or #9 cut. If you plan to rotary cut your strips, a #8 ($^1/_4$"-wide) strip will be easy for you to measure, so I recommend starting there. To use a strip cutter, follow the directions provided by the manufacturer for your model. To cut strips with a rotary cutter, first make a snip near one corner of the fabric and tear away the edge to give you a clean grain line to start your cutting.

Basic Rug Hooking

Now that you've selected your equipment, transferred your design, and cut your wool strips, all the work is behind you. It's time to start the best and easiest part—the hooking. Don't worry if at first it seems a bit slow and tedious. Before long you will be comfortable with the technique and you will agree that this part is fun, rewarding, and relaxing. When I work with brand-new artists who are making their first piece, I am reminded of that early anxiety over the pulling of loops, and the feeling of being so slow and awkward that you think you will never get it. With a little practice you'll soon forget that you ever had reservations about hooking. You'll fall into your own rhythm and you'll notice improvement with each piece you hook.

How to Hook

I'm right-handed and the following directions are explained from my point of view. If you're left-handed, simply switch directions and hold the wool and hook in opposite hands from what I have indicated.

1. Put the backing fabric in your hoop or frame so it is taut.
2. Hold a strip in your left hand under the backing material.

Hooking by Number

This organizational technique is quite effective when working with different wool colors for similar images, such as the different off-whites I used in "White Stars Rug" (page 17). I set aside the amount of wool needed for each star, placed each color in a separate plastic bag, and marked a number on each bag. Then I used a permanent marker to write the numbers on the stars on my rug backing so I'd know just where to use each shade of off-white. It's a little like "hooking by number" but can be a big help on projects that call for similar designs in different or slightly different colors.

3. In your right hand, hold your hook as you would hold a pencil.

4. Poke the hook into the backing fabric and pull the wool strip through the backing so that the tail end pokes up through the fabric.

5. Repeat, this time pulling a loop. Pull it up to your desired-length loop, about ⅜" long. You may want to experiment a little until you find the correct loop length for you.

6. Continue pulling loops through the backing fabric until you come to the end of your wool strip. Then pull the tail up through the backing and snip the tail end to the length of your loops. (Keep a handheld vacuum or whisk broom close by for easy cleanup.)

7. When starting a new strip of wool, pull the tail end up into the same hole in which the previous strip ended and continue hooking.

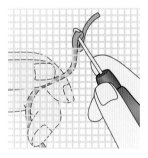

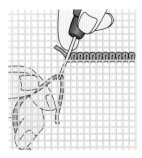

Tips for Hooking Success

When you are beginning the process of hooking and pulling loops, keep the following tips in mind and your rugs will turn out great.

- Keep the height of loops uniform, about ⅜" tall. Most beginners tend to not pull the loops up high enough. Concentrate on making nice, same-height loops from the start and you won't have to worry about changing or improving your style later on.

- Don't hook loops too close together. They can become disfigured and your finished rug might not lie flat. Skipping one or more holes in the weave of the backing fabric while hooking keeps the loops loose, yet fills in the surface quite nicely.

- Don't twist the wool strips. Use your hand below the backing material to keep the wool flat on the underside of the rug.

- Pull the tails through the backing and snip the end from the top side to keep the underside neat and prevent raveling.

- Hook inside the drawn lines. This keeps the images at the proper size. Going outside—even a little—can throw off an entire design.

- For a primitive-style rug, outline a shape such as an animal or flower first, and then fill in the shape. Outlining (again, done inside the drawn line) can be done in the same color wool as the rest of the image or in a slightly darker or contrasting color.

Getting Started

Hooking is generally started in the center of the rug where the primary design is located. Hook all of the motifs in the rug, and then go back and fill in the background areas. Finally, hook the border. Of course, there's an exception to every rule. On "Large Game Board Rug" pictured on pages 6 and 7, I hooked the border first! This rug is almost a room-sized rug, which meant I had to use the entire width of the linen backing fabric to accommodate the design. I felt that hooking the border first in this case would help stabilize the large piece of fabric.

The Importance of Color

I've said it before and I still believe it more than ever, some 325 rugs later—color is the most essential aspect of any rug. Technique is also important, but the colors in a rug make an impression on you before you even have a chance to look at the artist's technique. The overall design of a rug is important, but motifs and designs are purely a personal choice. You may prefer traditional, geometric, floral, or my love—folk-art designs. But whatever the style, if the color doesn't appeal to you or the placement of it is wrong, the rug just won't be pleasing to you. Even though I use fewer colors than most hookers, and muted colors at that, color is still key to me.

Time will not improve poor color placement in a rug, either. If you are working on a rug and a certain color you're using is bothering you, stop and move on to another part of the rug. Go back to the offending color in a day or two. If it still doesn't seem quite right, remove it. I was very hesitant to do this when I first started hooking rugs. I've gone back to a couple of rugs years later and pulled out the color that was troubling me, and I was sorry I waited so long to do it. It's easy to pull out the strips and replace them with another color— not like ripping out sewing mistakes!

Develop Your Own Color Sense

People tend to develop a signature in their rugs after a fashion, and often before the artists realize they have done so. Whether you like to hook a certain image, have a great sense for borders, or always use the same color palette, you're developing your own style. Color is a signature for many people. If you constantly use the same palette, that is part of your signature or style. My color choices are limited and I use muted shades— that is a trademark of mine.

You do not have to use all colors or have a flair for the brightest of colors or only dulled colors. Work in the colors you love, not just the colors I have presented in this book. When speaking to groups, I tell people to find the colors that they are happy with and embrace them—add different shades of your beloved colors and do not feel you have to use colors that you are not comfortable with. To determine your color palette, recognize the colors you love and use most often. Whether you are designing a rug, buying clothes, or decorating your home, you know that there are colors you go to quickly; these colors are the beginning of your personal color palette.

A New Perspective

As I hook often with friends, I pick up lots of tips by watching them and seeing how they manage their art. For instance, often I use a digital camera to take photos of my rugs as they progress. Seeing my rug from a different perspective helps me determine if the color and design arrangements are working properly.

Here are some of the tricks my friends use to see their rugs from a different viewpoint. One friend puts tacks on top of her mantel and occasionally hangs her rug in progress from the tacks so that she can stand back and see how it is looking from a distance. Another friend hangs her rug from her studio door with a skirt hanger at the end of the day. When she enters her studio the next morning with fresh eyes and sees her rug from a distance, she get a better feel as to how the colors are working.

Color Variations

To achieve the look of an antique rug or a well-loved folk-art piece, I like to use what I call "old colors"—colors that are grayed and dusky as opposed to bright and clear. In addition to starting with muted colors, I get the "old" look by collecting a variety of checks, plaids, stripes, and plain fabrics and overdyeing them together in a single dye formula. After the dye process, the strips are cut and randomly mixed in a basket. When a rug uses a blend of these strips, the end result is eye-catching color, depth, and texture, and I think it gives the rug motion. This technique creates a more authentic look than that of the same wools dyed separately. A perfect example of this principle in action is "White Stars Rug" on page 17. This rug could have been quite plain and two-dimensional if I had used just one blue wool and one off-white wool. But the mixture of many different blues and off-whites gives depth and drama to this two-color rug.

Borders

The choices for borders are truly endless, and again very personal. Not all rugs need to have a border (see "Irish Chain Rug" on page 85), and yet some rugs are truly distinctive because of their wonderful borders. If you examine antique rugs, you'll see that many of them don't have borders at all, while some have truly magnificent borders that are even more outstanding than the rugs themselves. Rugs are just like quilts—some have borders, and some are better off without.

When you're planning your project, try to visualize your rug design in its entirety before you begin, and decide at that time whether you are going to have a border. Of course, provided you have sufficient backing fabric and enough wool, you can make a change as you go along, but it is best to have the total rug in mind when you start.

Breaking the Rules

I have to admit that I recently broke one of my own border rules. I was working on a rug that I had fun planning—and thought it was thoroughly planned out. But when I got to the border I deviated from my plan and used a new color. I thought it would be a good choice, and I did love how the border was turning out. However, because I hadn't used this particular color earlier in the rug, my wonderful border didn't really seem to "belong" when the rug was finished. I decided I had to add the border color to the center of the rug in some fashion. I ended up pulling out some of the background loops here and there and substituting the border color I loved. The result was a whimsical polka-dotted background. This experience taught me to use my imagination and be creative. You can do it too!

Finishing Your Rug

From binding techniques to blocking, signing, and caring for your rug, here are the basics for finishing your rug.

Binding

If you are very careful in the binding of your rug, any of the following methods will be fine. Simply use the method you like best.

Rug-binding tape: This method was used on most antique rugs, which is appealing to me, so it's a technique that I use frequently. It's faster than whipstitching the edges with yarn (see page 139) and also makes a nice

finish. You can apply the binding tape to the backing in one of two ways.

Using a sewing machine, stitch the edge of the tape to the rug backing before you start to hook. That way you can hook right up to the sewn edge and have no backing fabric showing. The other way is to sew the binding tape on by hand after the rug has been hooked, sewing close to the edge of the rug and the tape. It's too hard to get close enough to the wool loops with a sewing machine after the rug is hooked. Either way, the binding will finish off your rug nicely.

After hooking is complete, trim the backing fabric to about 1" all the way around the rug. Then fold the binding tape over the cut edge of the backing and hand sew the tape to the back of the rug.

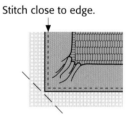

Stitch close to edge.

Trim corner to eliminate bulk.

Vintage fabric strips: I often bind my rug with vintage fabric, and ticking (striped, canvas-weight fabric) is my favorite choice. You will see vintage ticking peeking out at the edges of some of my rugs in this book; this is a look that I like. Striped pillow ticking is fairly easy to find, and it is sturdy, inexpensive, and gives the rugs a great look. To apply fabric, cut the strips 2" to 2½" wide, fold the strips in half lengthwise, and sew the raw edges of the fabric to the rug edges after hooking is complete. Trim the excess rug backing fabric, fold the strips to the back of the rug, and hand sew in place just as for binding tape.

Whipstitched edges: Many people "whip" the edges of their rug, folding back the edges of the backing fabric and stitching them in place with woolen yarn. The result is nice looking, but I find it time-consuming (perhaps because I do not sew). I've never seen an antique rug finished in this fashion, so I've never felt compelled to use it myself.

Wool strips: Another way to finish a rug is to use the strips of wool that you hooked into the rug. If you used larger strips, such as a #8 or #9 cut, you may need to cut them in half so they will fit in a needle. Thread the wool strips into a large needle and sew the edge of the rug to the back side with wool strips.

Braiding: If you happen to be a rug braider, you can use that skill for finishing your hooked rugs. It is a look that I love and that was seen often on early rugs. It is also a good way to extend the size of a hooked rug. I am not a rug braider, but I have a friend who is. You can always trade favors or hire someone to do this for you if you like the finish. For a coordinated look, use some of the same wool for the braiding as was used in your hooked rug.

After hooking is complete, finish the edges with binding tape. Then hand sew the braided strips to the edge of the rug.

Facing: For a rug with irregularly shaped edges such as the "Patriotic Shield Rug" (page 69), it's easier to finish the edges with a facing rather than with binding tape or binding strips. To make a facing, lay the facing fabric on top of the rug so that right sides are facing. Pin in place. On the wrong side of the rug, machine stitch around shape of the rug as close to the edge of the rug as possible. Then carefully trim away the center portion

of the fabric, leaving about 3" of facing fabric all around the perimeter. Take care to not cut into your loops!

Clip corners and points so that they will not bunch or pucker when the facing is turned. Turn facing to the back side of the rug, turn under the raw edges, and stitch them in place to the rug backing fabric.

New Designs

Long before you're finished hooking your rug, let alone binding and blocking it, your mind will be thinking of the next rug. Don't let your creative ideas escape. I have learned to jot down an idea as soon as it comes into my head—and I usually do so on the back of my checkbook, as that is probably the most important item in my purse and I won't be losing it. Another idea is to keep a small notebook in your purse. Then when you travel, spend time waiting for an appointment, or watch your children's sporting events, you can quickly jot down the essence of an idea or make a sketch while the concept is fresh in your mind. You can always improve on it when you have time, but don't lose the thought.

Blocking

Lay your hooked rug flat on the floor. If it's been pulled out of shape quite a bit, pull it as straight as you can and use long T-pins to secure the rug to your carpet or area rug. Wet a towel (or more than one for a large rug) and lay it on top of the rug. Using a steam iron, press the towel over the rug until you feel the rug is completely flat. If necessary, adjust the rug again while still damp. Pull out the pins, stretch the rug again, and re-pin. Reposition the damp towel and press over the entire surface until the rug is just slightly damp. Remove the towel and leave the rug pinned down to dry overnight. In the morning you will have a nicely shaped rug.

Signing Your Rug

It is important to sign your rug. Most often, rug hookers will hook their initials and date into the corner of the rug or actually work them into the design in a clever way. If you want to sign your rugs on the surface, hook your name or initials and the date where you want them in any color wool. This is merely to hold the space for the information. Then, as you near completion of the rug, determine whether the color you selected for the signature is the one you want to keep. If you want to change the color, pull out the loops and replace them with your new color. This makes the task so much easier than trying to hook the information later when surrounding loops are in place.

Another way to document your rugs is to make a fabric label and hand sew it to the back of the rug. This is how I sign all of my rugs. Include the name of the rug on your label, the date you hooked it, your name if you designed it (or the name of whoever did design it), who you made the rug for, and your signature. Most of my labels are in the shape of stars. If the rug is hemmed with black binding tape, the star is sewn onto a piece of black fabric to coordinate. For rugs hemmed with vintage ticking, the star is sewn onto the ticking. When it comes to labeling, my advice is twofold: always sign your rugs and be creative in finding a method that is uniquely suited to you and your style of rugs.

Caring for Your Rug

Hooked rugs are durable. History shows us that. Just consider all the hooked rugs and quilts that you have admired over the years. These time-proven works of art are more than a feast for the eyes; they were made for use and comfort, and if well cared for they can endure for well over 100 years. So if you

take good care of your rugs, they can last a very long time.

The biggest enemy to hooked rugs is water, so do not wash them or get them wet after they have been hooked. This might seem like odd advice, because I have already talked about washing your wool in a machine to prevent moths from feasting on it, and boiling it in a dye kettle to change the color. But that goes for individual pieces of wool and is where the use of water ends. After a rug has been hooked, washing it could make the colors run or mix. Keep this in mind before placing a rug near your sink or tub.

Hooked rugs do need to be kept clean; you just don't want to wash them. Sand and dirt left in the fibers can be abrasive and cause damage to the wool strips. The best way to clean a hooked rug is with an electric broom. Most home vacuums are too strong for hooked rugs and can lift them right off the floor, pulling out some loops. You can take your rugs outside occasionally and gently shake them. If a rug becomes stained, it's best to mix up mild soap flakes, sponge the suds onto your rug, and then brush off the surface with a damp sponge. I find that brushing a rug with a slightly damp sponge can pick up animal hairs also. Don't worry—a damp sponge cannot hold enough water to make the color run.

When we lived in Michigan, my neighbor shared a great idea for cleaning rugs. Take your rugs outside on a winter day with freshly fallen snow, gently shake the rugs, and then place them right-side-down on the snow for a bit. Pick them up and brush them off. The dampness of the snow works great for cleaning the rug surface; but now that we are in sunny southern Florida, I can't use that method anymore.

I have hooked rugs all over our house. With a pet Airedale in residence, as well as seven grandkids who visit often, our rugs get lots of use. My rugs are much more durable than most people imagine. We even have several hooked rugs in our master bath, near the tub and shower. We just take care not to splash them or soak them. Always respect your rugs and you won't have problems.

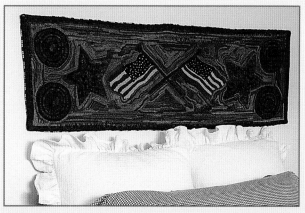

Resources

For quilting and rug-hooking equipment and supplies, check with your local fabric store or contact one of the companies listed below.

Rug-Hooking Supplies

Blackberry Primitives
1944 High Street
Lincoln, NE 68502
402-421-1361
402-423-8464
www.blackberryprimitives.com
A large selection of overdyed and textured wools, plus necessary tools

Dorr Mill Store
PO Box 88
Guild, NH 03754
800-846-3677
www.dorrmillstore.com
Wool yardage, direct from the mill, as well as other hooking supplies

Kindred Spirits
115 Colonial Lane
Kettering, OH 45429
937-435-7758
www.kindredspiritsdesigns.com
Hand-dyed wool; rug backing; hooks, hoops, and frames; rotary-cutting system; and other supplies

Ott-Lite Technology
1214 West Cass Street
Tampa, FL 33606
www.ott-lite.com
Manufacturer of Ott-Lite TrueColor lighting available in table, floor, and task lights

W. Cushing & Company
PO Box 351
Kennebunkport, ME 04046
800-626-7847
www.wcushing.com
Dyes and supplies for overdyeing wool

The Wool Studio
Rebecca Erb
706 Brownsville Road
Sinking Spring, PA 19608
610-678-5448
www.thewoolstudio.com
Great source for "as-is" wool

Cutters

Harry M. Fraser Co.
PO Box 939
Stoneville, NC 27948
336-573-9830
www.fraserrugs.com
Fraser Model 500-1 and Bliss Cutting Machines

Rigby Precision Products
PO Box 158
Bridgton, ME 04009
207-647-5679
Rigby Cloth Stripping Machine

Townsend Industries, Inc.
Box 97
Altoona, IA 50009
877-868-3544
email: t-51info@t-51.com
Townsend Fabric Cutter

Publications

The Wool Street Journal
312 N. Custer
Colorado Springs, CO 80903
888-784-5667
www.woolstreetjournal.com
Quarterly magazine for rug hookers

Rug Hooking Magazine
1300 Market Street, Suite 202
Lemoyne, PA 17032
800-233-9055
Published five times a year

Quilting Supplies

Martingale & Company
20205 144th Ave. NE
Woodinville, WA 98072
1-800-426-3126
www.martingale-pub.com
Papers for foundation piecing

Utica Thread Co., Inc.
602 Merrick Road
Lynbrook, NY 11563
888-UTICA-CO (888-884-2226)
www.uticathread.com
Silk quilting thread

YLI Corporation
161 West Main Street
Rock Hill, SC 29730
803-985-3100
www.ylicorp.com
Cotton quilting thread and YLI Select thread for hand piecing

Hobbs Bonded Fibers
200 South Commerce Drive
Waco, TX 76710
254-741-0040
www.hobbsbondedfibers.com
Heirloom Organic quilt batt without scrim

Acknowledgments

Both Polly and Laurie would like to thank:

- The entire staff of Martingale & Company for their support and encouragement. We feel blessed to have such expertise and unflagging commitment in our corner. Thanks to everyone.
- Frito-Lay, Inc., for their valuable time and help and for allowing us to use their logo in creating our baseball projects.
- A special thanks to Rita Barnard and Davey DeGraff for being able to take our amateur sketches and know exactly what we were trying to get across. Their help in getting our ideas onto fabric is always appreciated.

In addition, Polly would like to thank:

- My family: Jeff, John, and Jim, along with Linda, Sharon, and Heidi for their support and love. They always make me think that "I can do anything."
- Our special and loving grandkids: Grant, Shelby, Rachel, Thomas, Emily Kate, Allison, and Michael, who continue to be my inspiration and joy. Time I can spend with this group is my most favorite time of all!
- And a very special thank-you to my husband, Tom, for always supporting and encouraging me and for being willing to help out in any way he can—which often means steaming and blocking the rugs!
- Our cousin, Patty Tracey, for letting us interpret one of her wonderful early textiles—and for being my lifelong friend who is always there when I need her.

- Luanne Lea for her willingness to drop anything and hem a rug. Her beautiful work has added much to the book, and I value her friendship.
- And to Laurie, who makes this all fun!

Laurie wishes to thank:

- My family, Bill and Lorelei, who are my biggest cheerleaders. A special thanks to Bill, who is always willing to help in any way he can and has driven me to every quilt shop in the Midwest.
- Linda Brannock, Jan Patek, and Gerry Kimmel Carr of Red Wagon for giving me permission to use the image of children sledding from their *Snow Bound* book in the border of my "Snow Day Quilt."
- And to Polly, for believing I could before I did.

In Memory

I would like to remember our Airedale, Dixie, who was my constant companion as I made all the rugs in this book. We were so saddened by her passing this year. Thanks to Marilyn Schmit for this adorable needlepunch pin, made by Victoria Ingalls.

Polly

About the Authors

Polly Minick

Laurie Simpson

Polly Minick

Polly and her husband of more than 40 years have three grown sons and seven grandchildren. Today, Polly and her husband, Tom, share their home in Naples, Florida, with their new Airedale, Annie.

Polly began hooking rugs in the late 1970s when her sons were in high school. Since then, her rugs have met with praise from all, thanks to stories of her work in various national publications. Articles in the magazines *Country Home, Better Homes and Gardens, American Patchwork & Quilting, Colonial Home, Coastal Living, Architectural Digest,* and *Victoria* have greatly enhanced her status. The *New York Times, Houston Chronicle,* and *Georgetowner* have also written of Polly's achievements.

Like early-American rug hookers, Polly draws inspiration from her love of home, family, nature, and country. This shows in her imagery, which includes houses, horses, hearts, flags, stars, and birds. Her patriotic works were particularly inspired when her son Jim was commissioned as an officer in the US Marine Corps; he is currently serving as a lieutenant colonel.

The ambiguity of Polly's motifs and patterns is understandable given her aim to preserve in the rugs her "naïve" quality. Her style is commonly described as "primitive, almost childlike," which places strong emphasis on her respect and solemn appreciation for early-American creations.

Polly's enthusiasm and expertise as a collector of Americana and her national acclaim as a creator of primitive-style hooked rugs have elevated Polly to being a guest lecturer. Various assemblies of fiber-artists' guilds have requested her commentary, and to date, she has lectured in more than 20 states.

For Polly, one of the benefits of authoring this book was the enjoyment of working with her sister, Laurie. In addition, she is excited about promoting fiber art as a true art form and encouraging others to follow her lead.

Laurie Simpson

For more than 30 years Laurie Simpson has delighted others with her quilts. Her work graces galleries and private collections and has been featured in *Country Home, Coastal Living, Architectural Digest,* and *American Patchwork & Quilting.*

A patchwork quilt in a magazine inspired Laurie to take up quilting when she was 14. Drawn to traditional themes and techniques, she pieces, appliqués, and quilts exclusively by hand. "I quilt in the car and at hockey games. Handwork is calming and meditative. It's the way I was meant to work," says Laurie.

Laurie lives with her husband, Bill, in Ann Arbor, Michigan. They share their home with a happy menagerie of three cats and a dog.